THE WOMAN WHO KNOCKED OUT SUGAR RAY

The Woman Who Knocked Out Sugar Ray

Ralph Dranow

ARROWHEAD PRESS / BERKELEY

This book was produced by Sandy Darlington.
Cover photo and design by Julie Reynolds, © 1982.
The cover photo was taken in *Rita's Senator Club* in Santa Cruz.
Models for the photo were: Lezlie, Glen Hill, Paul Christmann,
    Carla Kandinsky, and Ralph Dranow.
Photo of author by Paul Christmann.

Library of Congress Cataloging in Publication Data

Dranow, Ralph.
   The woman who knocked out Sugar Ray.

   I. Title.
PS3554.R2377W6   1982   813'.54   81-70081
ISBN 0-9604152-5-4

Our books are distributed by *Book People* and by
    Publishers Group West.

Or you can get this book by sending $4.95 to:

     Arrowhead Press
     3005 Fulton
       Berkeley, California   94705

     (415) 548-5110

CONTENTS

The Woman Who Knocked Out Sugar Ray   1
Serious and Silly   19
The Second American Revolution   28
The Saga of Gertrude Pinsky   39
The Playground   54
No, I Mean He's a Negro   72
The Afghanistan Situation   88
Berkeley Rendezvous   93
The Ballad of Joe Hill   106
The Writing Block   128
Nirvana on a Summer Afternoon   136
Adventures of a Temporary   149

Chapters III and XVI from Dranow's
novel, *The Boric Acid Kid*:

Grandma Anna   162
Mickey   170

This book is dedicated to Carla and to my parents,
Rachel and Abraham Dranow, for making it possible.

THE WOMAN WHO KNOCKED OUT SUGAR RAY

HARVEY TEITELBAUM DRUMMED his foot on the floor, his small, deep-set eyes blinking incessantly as he hurled words at me. We were sitting at a table drinking beer in Stanley's, a bar on 12th Street and Avenue B. It was Friday night, September 1961, and Harvey would soon be starting grad school at Brooklyn College, while I had just filed a C.O. application with my local draft board. "Now you're primarily concerned with staying out of the army. Right?" Harvey demanded. "So the simplest, most logical way to do that, obviously, is to stay in school. It's a great justification for your existence. Even if I'm still in school when I'm 30, as long as it looks as if I'm plodding toward some sort of higher degree, I'll be considered a respectable citizen, people will leave me alone. . . . Figure it this way. At home I'll be getting my meals and laundry done free, as well as a place to sleep, and all I have to do for that is register for a few courses each term and do just enough work to keep from getting kicked out. But on the other hand, if you try to become a C.O., then people will notice you, you're asking for trouble. And either way you lose. If you don't get C.O. status, you'll end up going into the army, anyway. And if you do become a C.O., then you'll be washing bedpans in some hospital somewhere, which would be at least as boring and meaningless as the army. So why try to be a hero?"

I shook my head impatiently. "Look, I'm not trying to be a hero or anything, but I wouldn't be happy faking my way through years of grad school. I do have certain ideals and principles, you know."

Harvey's gray eyes twinkled sardonically. "Usually it's the people who talk the most about ideals and principles who turn out to be the biggest perpetrators of evil," he informed me. "It's the self-righteous types who take themselves too seriously that you have to watch out for."

"You're too cynical, Harvey," I retorted. "Actually, I bet you yourself don't believe even half of what you say."

Twitching his pug nose in an ironic smile, Harvey ran nervous fingers through his dark crewcut. "On a cosmic level it doesn't really matter whether I'm sincere or not," he declared. "It's all relative, anyway. The point is, everything we've been discussing is totally insignificant in the final scheme of things."

I sighed. "All right. Let's drop the whole subject."

Harvey shrugged and took a long swallow of beer. We sat sipping from thick glass mugs and carefully avoiding each other's eyes. It had been fun hanging around and playing tennis with Harvey throughout our Queens College years, but now that our lives were at a more serious stage, I felt increasingly alienated by Harvey's cynicism, his man-of-the-world pose. Behind this facade, he was like me, just a scared, virginal college grad who wasn't really sure how he felt about most things.

Both of us had taken to observing other people in

the dim light of the noisy, crowded bar, which had an
air of seedy elegance about it. Large, round chandeliers
hung from the square-molded ceiling; and there was an
antique clock on the wall opposite the bar. Each table
possessed a slightly frayed red and white checkered table-
cloth and a small, round lantern containing a candle; an
impressive array of bottles glinted invitingly from behind
the black oak bar. Stanley's was acquiring a reputation
as a place to hang out for bohemians and intellectuals,
and I hungered to get to know people here, imagining
them to be living exciting, creative lives. There were
several attractive women, and though none of them seem-
ed to take particular notice of me, still, I nurtured hopes
of at least getting to talk to one of them before night's
end. The antique clock indicated it was just past ten,
which meant there was still plenty of time for something
interesting to happen. I was feeling pleasantly tipsy and
in a mood to cast aside my usual inhibitions.

Harvey broke our silence, making wry speculations
about various people in the bar, such as whether they
were genuine artists or just pretenders, and whether they
had some secret, illicit occupation. It was an absorbing
game, and I realized once again why I had stayed friends
with Harvey for so long. Fortunately, the din of conver-
sation and the music from the juke box, Billie Holliday
singing *Lover Man*, were loud enough to prevent anyone
from overhearing us. "Basically, this place is just a mena-
gerie of misfits," Harvey summed up, as he rocked back
and forth in his chair.

A squat, light-skinned black woman wearing dark
glasses shambled over to our table. A sweet fragrance
trickled into my nostrils, as her round face eased into a
sleepy smile. "Hello, beautiful," she said to me in a deep,
gravelly voice. "I don't think I've seen you in here be-
fore, have I?"

I blushed. "No, I guess not. This is our first time
here."

"Far out! Where are you cats from?"

"Fargo, North Dakota," Harvey mumbled.

"We're from Flushing," I said loudly, hoping she hadn't heard Harvey.

She looked puzzled. "Flushing? Where the fuck is that?"

"It's in Queens. . . . You know where Queens College is?" I asked.

She nodded slowly. "Yeah, now I get the picture. Two college boys out to lose their cherries. Am I right?" Her abundant frame in tight black slacks and red cotton blouse quivered with hoarse, raucous snorts and wheezes.

"Jesus Christ!" Harvey muttered, turning pale and shooting me a pained look. I merely grinned and shrugged in reply.

After a few final rasping sputters of mirth, the black woman said, "Pardon me. Sometimes I get a little bit raunchy. Anyway, if you cats don't mind I'll join you when I come back from the john."

Harvey and I watched her negotiate a rather fluctuating path to the bathroom. When she'd disappeared inside, Harvey slowly shook his head. "Lovely creature! I wonder where they dredged her up from. That's 200 pounds of solid, rippling muscle."

I wasn't amused. "All right, so maybe she weighs about 160 pounds or so. Anyway, what do you have against her?"

He laughed perfunctorily. "Is that a serious question? Well, for starters she's a drunken, foul-mouthed whore, and she isn't even pretty. So if you want to talk to her, go ahead, but I think I'll decline the honor." He stood up.

"Are you leaving?"

"Yeah. Why? You ready to go?"

I hesitated. Perhaps our friendship is at stake now, I reflected. Besides, Harvey has a car. If things don't work out with her, I'll have to take the subway home by myself, and I'm not familiar with this neighborhood at all.

"Well?" Harvey demanded, putting on his white zippered tennis jacket. In his jacket, tennis shoes, and tan chinos, he looked very collegiate.

"I think I'll stay," I said, deciding I was in the mood to gamble.

Harvey shrugged. "All right. Suit yourself, then. See you around."

He wheeled and started toward the door. I watched his short, wiry body brush past clots of people, chin upraised, shoulders thrust back, as if he were engaged in a crucial tennis match observed by a multitude. Then, with a stiff gesture, he flung open the door and disappeared into the night. "You self-righteous bastard! You white middle-class turd!" I muttered under my breath.

The black woman lumbered toward me, plopping herself down in the seat Harvey had vacated. "What happened to your friend?" she inquired.

"He left."

She gave me her slow, lazy grin. "Well, I honestly can't say I'm too sorry. He didn't seem very friendly."

"I guess he's kind of scared of women," I said.

In reply, her stare appraised me unhurriedly. Self-consciously, I tried to meet her eyes through the wall of her dark glasses. She looked odd, even a bit sinister, almost like a Samurai warrior with her hard face and pencilled eyebrows slanting upwards over her glasses. Her wide, full mouth was a bright red, and large white hoops descended from her earlobes. She's probably an interesting racial mixture, I thought.

"And you? Aren't you scared of me?" she asked at last.

I felt my knees shaking underneath the table, and my palms oozed, but I managed to keep my voice under control. "No, why should I be?"

She threw back her head and laughed abruptly. "Because I'm big, black, drunk as hell, and old enough to be your mother."

My knees still trembled. "That's all right with me,"

I said determinedly.

She scrutinized me once more, very briefly this time, then said, "I like you. Even though you look a little bit square, you're probably as weird as me. What's your name?"

"Steve Maltz. What's yours?"

"Gloria Brown."

We shook hands, and then Gloria said, "Let's split. My pad's right near here."

"Fine," I managed.

She got to her feet a bit shakily. "I sincerely hope I'm not too loaded to appreciate you tonight, baby," she drawled.

I nodded nervously and put on my gray cotton jacket. We went toward the door. "Later," Gloria said, winking and waving goodbye to her friends at the bar. I felt their eyes focused curiously on me and felt extremely self-conscious.

Outside it was still rather warm and muggy as we went down Avenue B, past closed stores and tenements with fire escapes jutting from them. Gloria was weaving about, and I suddenly wondered whether I really wanted to go home with her. Instead of being with a young, pretty, educated sort of woman, here I was with an odd-looking, tough-talking drunk who was probably at least twice my age.

"Look . . . you know, maybe tonight isn't a good time, . . " I began.

"I figured you might get cold feet sooner or later," Gloria cut in. "Well, I don't know that I really blame you. Anyway, just come over here a minute."

When I did so, she clasped her arms around me and insinuated her tongue into my mouth. I'd kissed a few girls before, but it had never felt like this. Her tongue slithered over mine, caressing it again and again until I was helplessly lightheaded, developing a sizeable erection. I was afraid I might go off right then and there when Gloria mercifully released me. She sighed deeply and exclaimed, "Wow! You'e too much, baby!"

"Maybe tonight is the right time," I said.

She exploded into laughter, almost losing her footing. When she'd recovered, she said, "Far out! I might be smashed, but I can still make that pecker of yours snap to attention."

Gloria took my hand, and we walked a little further until we came to a shabby-looking, white, four-story building. She took out some keys from a small black change purse and after a moment or two of fumbling got the front door open. We proceeded carefully up the creaking stairs. The hallway was dark and musty, permeated by the stench of urine, cheap wine, and stale cooking odors. On the fourth floor Gloria wrestled with the double lock, accompanying her strenuous efforts with loud sighs and fierce growls. I was beginning to think we'd have to settle for the hallway when the door finally gave way. A light was on, and I was struck immediately by the complete disorder prevailing in the living room. Everything from broken chair legs and empty beer bottles to pieces of jewelry and old, discarded clothes was scattered about. A parrot was chattering away in a cage, and Gloria went over to it, snapping her fingers and shaking her body, as she cooed, "Whip it on me, Sonny baby! Whip it on me!"

"Yes, yes, yes," the bird jabbered in reply, hopping about excitedly.

Gloria repeated her invitation several more times, generally eliciting an enthusiastic response from Sonny. Then I was rewarded with another delectable kiss before I felt Gloria breaking away. "I'll be right back, I've got to go to the john," she said.

With my head in orbit, I watched her stumble to the bathroom. Then I sat down on an old, faded sofa and glanced around the apartment. In addition to assorted pieces of furniture in varying states of disrepair, I observed a Ouija board, several books by Kahlil Gibran, records by Duke Ellington, Ella Fitzgerald, and Frank Sinatra. I

was pleasantly surprised by Gloria's having books in her
apartment and began feeling curious about her. Who is
she, really? And why did she select me? I asked myself.
Then I remembered something and groaned. It was after
11:30. I should call my mother and tell her I won't be
home tonight, I thought. Otherwise, who knows what
sort of wild ideas she'll come up with!

My mother answered on the second ring. "Hi, Ma.
Look," I began.

"Where are you, Steve? Is everything all right?"
she asked anxiously.

"Yeah, everything's O.K. . . . . I'm staying over at a
friend's house tonight. . . . . I'll be home sometime to-
morrow."

There was a pause. Then she demanded, "Who are
you staying with? What happened to Harvey?"

"Look, Ma, don't worry. Harvey went home, and
I'm staying with a friend in Manhattan. I. . . . . "

"Just give me the phone number, then, so I can get
in touch with you if I need to."

I winced. I didn't want my mother hearing Gloria's
strange, hoarse voice on the phone and wondering what
kind of weirdo she was. "Look, you won't need to call
me," I told her. "Anyway, I have to hang up now."

"Well, I hope she's nice, Steve. Maybe I'll get to
meet her eventually."

"Yeah, O.K. So long." I hung up just as my mother
was starting to tell me to be careful.

I sighed, wondering whether she would ever cease
worrying about me, then began laughing. If my mother
only knew, she'd have a fit, I mused. Gloria isn't exactly
her idea of a nice Jewish girl, or a nice Gentile one for
that matter. Then I realized that Gloria had been in the
bathroom for quite some time, so I went and rapped on
the door. No answer. I knocked again, louder.
"Gloria? . . . Are you in there?" I yelled. Complete
silence. Damn it! Why the hell did I ever get myself
into this! I asked myself. Maybe she's fallen down and

split her head open or something. When I pounded and called out once more, still getting no reply, I tried the door handle. The door jerked open, and I just stood there, gaping. Snoring softly, Gloria straddled the toilet seat, glasses riding the broad wings of her nose, a blissful expression pervading her face. Her slacks and bikini underpants were down at her ankles, and I felt myself getting hard as I blinked at the large, strong, tan thighs cradling a jungle of black pubic hair. I wanted to laugh at the absurdity of the whole situation, but my exasperation outweighed my amusement. Now what?

"Gloria, wake up!" I entreated.

Lips parted, Gloria went on snoring, a full-bellied toilet seat Buddha with dangling sunglasses.

"Gloria, please, wake up for heaven's sake!" I shook her lightly.

"Huh?" She opened her eyes a crack and peered bewilderedly at me over her glasses.

"You fell asleep on the toilet seat."

"Yeah, I know. Sorry." Her eyes slid shut.

Sighing deeply, I considered leaving now, then decided to give it one more try. The promise of her kisses, the nearness of her nakedness excited me. "Gloria, listen!"

Her eyes squeezed open when I vigorously shook her arm. "Yeah? What do you want?" she demanded drowsily.

"Look, I could leave now if you'd like."

Her yawn seemed to take forever, as I stared stupidly into the pink cavern of her throat. She made a heroic effort to focus on me. "I'll be O.K. in the morning. I'm sorry, honey. I'd like you to stay, but if you want to split, that's cool."

I considered a moment, then said, "All right. I'll stay. Do you want me to help you into bed?"

"Yeah. Thanks. Just pull my pants off first." Her head drooped, and her eyes closed again. Probably this wasn't the first time this sort of thing had happened to her.

I removed her glasses and shoes, then rolled her slacks and panties off. I stood her up, managing with great effort to coax her out of the bathroom and into bed. I threw a sheet over her, and after a muffled thanks, she was almost immediately snoring again. Asleep, and without her dark glasses, her face looked gentler, like that of a large, serene tomcat. I watched her for a while, shaking my head over the weird situations I managed to get myself into. Harvey, of course, would think I was absolutely crazy. I tried to sleep but felt restless and hungry, so I got up and went to the refrigerator. Opening it, I was greeted by several cans of beer, a little bit of wine, and a container of milk that had gone bad. Shrugging, I slammed the door and went into the living room. Soon I was immersed in Gibran's *The Prophet*, stirred by its lyrical fusion of social consciousness, earthiness, and spirituality. It rekindled my desire to become a writer, to embrace all sorts of new, transcendant experiences. When I'd finished the book several hours later, sleepily and contentedly I stretched out beside Gloria, whose undulating body was gently stirring the sheet covering her.

In the morning I finally entered what Gibran would call paradise. Gloria was patient with me as I fumbled with her generous body like an overeager schoolboy. When I had been about this for quite a while, I gave her an urgent, perplexed look, and she roared with laughter. She guided me inside her, then wrapped her legs around me, moving strenuously in contrast to my own tentative rhythms. Underneath me, she was like a Mack truck attempting furiously to shift into high gear. Then I couldn't hold back any longer the fluttery, tantalizing explosion mounting inside me, and Gloria gave a loud moan and dug her heels into my sweaty, trembling back. I felt grateful to Gloria, as if I could stay here in this bed forever, making love with her. We lay locked in each other's arms, and it felt voluptuous and comforting nestled in the harbor of her full, warm body. Then Gloria moved away to light a cigaret. She puffed reflectively on it, letting the smoke ease lazily out of her wide nostrils.

"What kind of work do you do?" I asked hesitantly.

She sighed. "Whatever I can hustle up. I've been doing some temporary office work lately. Once upon a time, though, I used to be a dancer and a damned good one, too. I danced with some of the top bands. Count Basie used to say that I danced like a snake, you know, like I had no bones in my body at all." There was a wistful expression on her face.

"No wonder your legs are so strong," I said, impressed by her past, by the realization that she must once have had a magnificent body. "But how come you're not still dancing?"

Gloria gave me a pitying look. "Child, I'm an old lady now. Anyway, 43 is old in the world of dancing. Hell, I can still dance just about like I used to, but they prefer the young chicks, you know. *C'est la vie.*"

"Yeah, that's too bad," I agreed.

Then, after a short silence, I asked, "Have you ever been married?"

Her somber expression vanished. "Yeah. Once. It lasted only three years. He always used to lay in bed and read physics books and play with his balls. You try to talk to him while he was readin' one of those damn physics books, and it was like talkin' to the wall. Besides, he used to have so much fucking wax in his ears you needed a cannon to blast the shit out."

We both laughed heartily.

"Was that in New York you were married?" I asked.

"No, in Boston. That's where I'm from. You know, I went to the same high school there as Sugar Ray Robinson. I even knocked him out once."

I stared at her. "Really?"

"Yeah, no shit. We were just runnin' our mouths, you know, kind of jivin' around, and I took a swing at him. The next thing you know Sugar Ray's lyin' on the ground out stone cold. Like I didn't even think I'd hit

him that hard. So dig this scene. All the dudes were runnin'
around the place hollerin', 'Hey, a broad knocked out
Sugar Ray! A broad knocked out Sugar Ray!'' Burbles
of laughter poured from Gloria's throat.

I'd believed Gloria's other two stories, but I wasn't
sure about this one. "How long was Sugar Ray out cold?"
I asked.

"Oh, I don't know, maybe a couple of minutes."

"You should have gone into the ring after that,"
I said.

Gloria chuckled. "Yeah, I was a real tiger back in
those days."

We made love again. I was a little less inept this
time, and afterwards Gloria said, "You know somethin'?
You're in trouble. I enjoy it. As long as you're willing
to put up with an old broad like me, you've got your-
self a date."

She lit a cigaret, and we talked some more. She
told me that her mother was white and her father black
with some Chinese blood. Gloria's mother, now dead,
had liked to read books and listen to classical music while
her father, a gambler, was tough and crude, she said.
They'd gotten divorced when she was a teenager.

I asked Gloria whether she'd ever read *The Prophet*.
She smiled. "That's my favorite book, man. That cat
Gibran is somethin' else. He gets right down to the nitty
gritty of things; that's a real deep dude if you ask me."

I agreed with Gloria in rather different language, of
course, then started telling her about my C.O. application.
I was a little disappointed when she merely shrugged and
said, "That's cool. We each have our own scene, I guess.
Hope you find what you're lookin' for. Anyway, how
about goin' out to hunt up some chow. I'm just about
starved."

We got dressed and left the apartment. It was late
morning, a beautiful, bright one, and I felt a sense of
satisfaction walking beside Gloria, who apparently was
my woman now. On 10th Street, we walked along

Tompkins Square Park, past old Ukrainians bundled in
sweaters as they hunched on benches or fed the pigeons;
past black and Puerto Rican youths exuberantly playing
basketball and handball; past young, hip-looking white
mothers overseeing their small children as they played.

On 9th Street and 1st Avenue, we went into a
small, unassuming-looking Ukrainian restaurant with a
long, winding counter surrounded by several tables. The
place was packed, but we grabbed a free table that some-
one had just vacated. The clientele was a varied one,
with one or two other interracial couples, while the em-
ployees were predominantly older, sallow, tired-looking
Ukrainian men. While we waited for our breakfast,
Gloria exchanged greetings and small talk with some
bohemian-looking types. I liked being here with her,
feeling that I was becoming part of this neighborhood,
where interracial couples seemed to be considered parti-
cularly enlightened. I did wonder, though, whether some
people found us an odd combination. Gloria insisted on
introducing me to people as her son, which she immedi-
ately followed up with a robust belly-laugh. I generally
laughed, too, though I wasn't sure whether it was all
that funny.

When our breakfast arrived, a generous one of bacon
and eggs, fried potatoes, toast, orange juice and coffee,
we dug in. It was tasty, and I finished mine considerably
before Gloria, who every few minutes remembered a new
anecdote she had to tell me, after which she laughed so
hard that she was unable to eat for a while. When Gloria
had finally disposed of her food, I told her that I had to
go, then paid for our meal, which was quite inexpensive.
Outside, Gloria gave me another one of her patented
kisses, admonishing me not to become a stranger and let
too much time pass before calling her.

In an exhilarated daze, I made my way toward the
I.R.T. subway. Somehow I managed to take the right
combination of trains and bus leading to Flushing and
Parsons Boulevard, which felt like the end of the world

after the Lower East Side. While I sat on the subway and
bus, I couldn't help thinking that people could probably
tell that I had just been through a momentous experience.

At home, my mother was anxious to know about my
new friend, of course, but I was rather stingy in doling
out any information. I could just see the startled look
on my mother's face if I related the toilet seat episode,
or Gloria's story about Sugar Ray Robinson, or even her
age. I began wondering myself whether I would actually
call her. I had things to do; besides sex and a mutual
liking for *The Prophet*, what else did we really have in
common? But as much as I tried to absorb myself in
my reading, writing, and tennis playing, my thoughts
hovered helplessly over bountiful thighs locked against
my ribs; exotic flesh the color of light coffee shooting
maddening sensations into my fingertips and groin; and
Gloria's magic tongue, of course. I called her on Sunday
and made a date for Monday evening.

During the following two weeks, I got together
with Gloria several times. Usually I visited her in the
evening, staying overnight, and had breakfast with her
the next morning. Sometimes she was drunk when I
came to see her, but she always wore something seduc-
tive and smelled nice from perfume and a recent bath.
The sex we had was good, though occasionally Gloria
chided me for being too much in a hurry. I accepted the
fact that our conversations afterwards weren't exactly
sparkling. Gloria seemed to be stuck in the past, and she
repeated to me frequently Count Basie's remark about
how she'd danced like a snake, as well as the various
nicknames her admirers had bestowed upon her. Also,
I heard several slightly expanded versions of the Sugar
Ray Robinson story, plus additional tidbits about
Gloria's ex-husband, such as his rotten toenails. She
didn't seem curious about me at all, never asking me any-
thing about myself. I'd gotten into the habit of reading
a book after we'd made love and Gloria was drowsily
telling me another one of her tales. And once of twice

I left early in the morning before she was fully awake.

One weekday evening in late September before meeting Gloria, I was hurriedly finishing up another book by Gibran, whom I was starting to get tired of. What had previously seemed eloquent and profound now struck me as verging on the banal and sentimental. When I got to Gloria's, it was almost nine o'clock, an hour past our planned meeting time. I apologized, but Gloria looked distant and didn't seem to hear me. She was wearing a tight black dress and heels, and when I tried to touch her, she edged away from me. "Come on, I'm tired of hanging around here. Let's go out for a change," she snapped.

We walked, silently for the most part, to a bar on Third Avenue off St. Marks Place. A nearly full moon illuminated the hot, humid September night. Unlike Stanley's, the place seemed like an ordinary neighborhood bar, and the sparse clientele was mostly black or Puerto Rican. There were photographs of boxers and baseball players on the wall, and the juke box was blaring a song by Chuck Berry. I bought a beer for myself and vermouth for Gloria. As we turned to find a table, a stocky, dark-skinned black man sitting at the bar hissed the epithet, "Uncle Tom" at Gloria. I'd seen him previously in Stanley's with a white woman.

"Motherfucker!" Gloria retorted, beckoning him to the back of the bar.

I was afraid they might start swinging, but instead they sat down at a back table, their heated voices drowned out by the music, as they gestured vehemently, with grim, taut expressions. I watched them uneasily from a bar stool, sensing that the argument concerned me, though neither one glanced in my direction. Once again, Gloria reminded me of a thug, with her dark glasses and sinister eyebrows. I resisted a sudden impulse to get up and vanish. After a few minutes, Gloria returned to me, leaving her adversary sitting at the table, glowering at the wall.

"What did he want?" I asked.

She waved disdainfully. "Shit, I've known Mack ever since high school, and he hasn't changed a bit. He says that I shouldn't be with you, that I'm a white man's nigger. Well, who I'm with is my own fucking business, not his. Besides, I notice that he never turns down the opportunity to be with white chicks. Probably one of them just rejected him so that's why he's in such a foul mood. Shit!"

She signalled the bartender for a vermouth, downed it in one gulp, asked for another and promptly disposed of that one, too. Then, crisply snapping her fingers, she began dancing to the juke box music with angry, exaggerated thrusts of her body. The attention of everyone in the bar was riveted to the spectacle of this big woman gyrating about as if she were on center stage. Gloria ignored the laughter and sexual jokes a few of the onlookers directed at her. Obviously, she'd once been a very good dancer, but now there was something a little pathetic about her, about the quivering of her flabby arms, the swaying of her enormous ass. She didn't glance once at Mack, but I knew that the performance was meant for him. Though I admired Gloria's courage, I was also concerned that Mack might get belligerent again, as he sat watching her with a formidable scowl. Suddenly he jerked up and stalked past Gloria's writhing body, muttering under his breath as he swept out the door. I heaved a sigh of relief.

A moment or two later, Gloria stopped dancing. Uncomfortably, I watched as she silently put drink after drink away, insisting on paying for them herself. She shook her head stubbornly when I suggested leaving. I began wondering whether there was any truth to what Mack had said. Was I just using Gloria sexually? And did I think it made me hip to sleep with her because she was black? In the midst of my anguished soul-searching,

Gloria, lurching from her stool, snapped, "C'mon, let's split."

The moon poured its eerie light on us as we burst out of the bar. The thick night air had cooled off considerably, and gratefully, I filled my lungs full of it. "Fuck! No one tells Gloria what to do, I don't care who he is!" she declared, shaking her head back and forth as we went along St. Marks Place.

"I thought people were less prejudiced around here," I ventured.

Gloria laughed bitterly. "What sort of dream world have you been livin' in, honey? Some of the Negroes down here are racist as hell. A lot of Negro men hate white men, you know."

I nodded, suddenly feeling like a little boy playing at being a man with an older woman.

Back in her apartment, Gloria surprised me by suggesting we make love. Halfheartedly, I consented. I felt intensely aware of all her physical defects, seeing her as an ugly and run-down old woman. I fought off these harsh thoughts, but it was no use. After a long while, I lay sprawled on my side of the bed, sweaty, exhausted, defeated. There didn't seem to be anything to say, and I drifted into my own world, speculating about how my C.O. application was faring.

I was startled into attention by Gloria's sudden question. "Do you love me?"

I looked at her. "What did you say?" But already, her words, like an explosive, had made an impact inside my head.

"Do you love me?" she repeated, slightly louder, and I broke into a cold sweat. A vision of being married to Gloria swam before my eyes, and I blinked it frantically away.

"No," I heard myself saying quietly but distinctly.

"Please, don't say that!"

I hadn't quite expected the hurt in her voice, the

wounded look on her face. I swallowed hard, the crash-
ing of my heart resounding in my ears. "All right . . . I'm
sorry . . . maybe. I don't know," I stammered, comforted
by the small smile flickering over her round face.

"That's better. At least it doesn't make it sound
like you've made up your mind forever."

"Yeah, I shouldn't have sounded so definite," I apolo-
gized, wishing I could will myself to love Gloria. But all
I could feel was profound sadness welling up inside me.

A silence thick as a blanket had set in between us.
Finally, to ease the awkwardness, I made tentative efforts
to stroke her. This seemed to soothe Gloria, so my caresses
became less diffident. Soon she was fast asleep, breathing
tranquilly, her face free of pain now.

I lay staring at the ceiling, sighing and cursing my-
self. Damn it! Who would ever have guessed that Gloria,
so hard and tough on the outside, would practically admit
that she loved me? Women are a tricky business all right,
but still, I should have known better than to let things
drag on this long, I told myself. I've been greedy and self-
ish. There's no denying it. In a weird way, maybe I do
love Gloria but not in the sense I know she meant. I
watched her sleep for a while, lips slightly parted, making
the little sibilant snore she often did. I put on my clothes
and decided to write her a note. I thought of a quote
from *The Prophet*, beginning, "Your children are not
yours, but the world's. . . ", then discarded it as being
too corny. Instead, I just wrote, "Thanks for every-
thing, Gloria. I'm sorry." Then I kissed her lightly on
the forehead, making her stir briefly, and tiptoed out the
door and down the rickety stairs. The oppressive feeling
weighing me down was tempered by an exhilarating sense
of freedom.

SERIOUS AND SILLY

ELLIOT AND FRANCESCA were returning home
one fine summer evening after having consumed a piquant
Mexican meal in a nearby restaurant. Holding hands,
their eyes glowing, they were looking forward to spend-
ing a quiet romantic evening together and playing with
their two cats, Serious and Silly. Elliot opened their door
of their first floor Berkeley apartment; a huge creature
knocked him to the ground.

"Jesus Christ! What the hell was that?" he demanded,
strenuously disengaging himself from its furry embrace
and struggling to his feet.

"It's Serious . . . only a lot bigger," Francesca said.

"Yeah. And the other one's Silly . . . only a lot
bigger, too. My God! They're almost the size of lions
and tigers!"

Before Francesca could reply, Serious wailed pierc-
ingly and with great determination attached herself to

Elliot's right arm.

"Down, girl. Down, girl," he coaxed, finally managing to extricate his bruised arm.

"She's probably hungry. We better feed them right away," Francesca said.

"Yeah, like in about two seconds," he chortled, threading his way inside through a minefield of effusive hugs and shrill hellos.

"Good cat. Good cat," he chanted like a litany, carefully stroking their massive heads.

The cats' food bowls glistened nakedly up at him. The two felines circled his legs, their fierce yellow eyes and insistent yowls testifying to an immense hunger. He pulled open the cabinet and reached for a can. Hurriedly, Elliot opened the Seafood Dinner and spooned the dark, sticky contents into the food bowls. Twice he removed his hand from them just in time. Meanwhile, Francesca filled two larger bowls with Good Mews crunchies. First the soft stuff slid down the cats' throats; then the crunchies exploded like firecrackers between their fangs. The food was completely gone in about a minute. Then the cats proceeded to set up another mighty wail. Serious sprang up on the dinner table, which began to buckle, and Silly prowled the stove and counter next to the sink. They loomed menacingly above Elliot and Francesca.

He glanced at the clock on the coffee table and moaned. "Jesus, it's after nine already so Park And Shop's closed. And we don't have any more cans left."

Francesca opened the refrigerator and took out a container of beef liver. She flung down a large reddish-brown slab beside each of the bowls. The cats bounded to the floor and began devouring the liver. Elliot and Francesca watched, mesmerized, as if at some obscene spectacle.

"It's incredible. They look exactly the same as before. Just exactly . . . except for being bigger, of course," she said.

He nodded, scrutinizing the two creatures intently. Serious, the mother cat, was still a sleek gray and white with a pouting, sensual face. Her facial markings were duplicated as well, featuring a black speck, like a mustache, under her milky nose. Silly, her son, as before was almost all gray, except for the long white zipper running down his trim belly and the fleecy clergyman's collar enfolding his chin, neck, and collarbone. Like his smaller version and his mother also, he had a pinpoint mustache and an angular, aristocratic-looking face.

Francesca tossed the cats the remaining two pieces of liver, which disappeared almost instantly. Their prodigious appetites seemed appeased, however. They loped toward the sliding door opening onto the balcony.

"We'd better open the door for them. They probably have to go after all that food," Francesca said.

Elliot frowned. "Yeah, I know, but do you think we ought to? They'll scare the hell out of anyone who sees them."

"But they don't seem vicious or anything, Elliot. Besides, it's dark outside, so hopefully no one will notice."

He gave Francesca an incredulous look.

The cats, rearing on their hind legs now, started to thump at the glass partition. The glass reverberated loudly. "Yeah, I guess we better let them out," he said, quickly sliding open the door. The cats bolted into the night. With a fluid bound, each of them was over the balcony railing, then hurtling through high weeds, eluding Elliot's desperate attempt to follow them with his eyes.

Pacing back and forth in the suddenly empty-looking living room, he said, "Maybe they won't come back. You know, they probably don't like being all cooped up in here."

"Elliot, stop it! We're still their people. Of course they'll come back."

"Look," he blurted. "We've got to do something soon. Very soon. Otherwise they'll be eating us out of house and home. Besides, if someone sees them and calls the police, we could even get arrested. They might be dangerous, you know."

"Don't be silly, Elliot! They're still our old Serious and Silly. You saw how affectionate to us they were when we came home."

He laughed sardonically and said, "What about the Berkeley Dog and Cat Hospital? Do they have an emergency number at night?"

"Yes. If you call the regular number, you'll get the answering service. They'll put you in contact with one of the doctors if it seems like an emergency."

He looked up the number in the phone book, then dialed.

"Yes? This is the answering service," a woman's voice said.

"We have an emergency situation with our cats. We'd like to talk to a doctor right away."

"What sort of situation is it?"

Elliot hesitated. "Well, you see, our cats have kind of gotten . . . well, bigger. . . . A lot bigger."

"Bigger? Is that what you just said?"

"Yes. Look, they're gigantic . . . I mean like almost the size of lions now. . . . We want to know what to do about them."

There was a long pause. Then the voice said crisply, "I'm afraid we can't help you."

"Look, I'm telling you the truth. You probably think I'm crazy or something. I know this is unusual, but. . . ."

"I'd suggest that you call in the morning."

"Thanks ever so much, sweetheart," he muttered, slamming down the phone.

Francesca put her hand on his arm. "Take it easy, Elliot. Getting all excited won't help. Let me call Doris. She knows a lot about cats."

Elliot paced back and forth, gnawing on his fingers while the two women talked. Finally Francesca hung up and said, "Doris says she's never heard of anything like this."

THE SAGA OF GERTRUDE PINSKY

ONE BALMY SATURDAY AFTERNOON in the spring of 1959, I was up in my room grappling with a paper on the mating habits of fruit flies. The teacher of the course was Malcolm Doakes, a senile old pedant who was a great stickler for the correct headings on his quizzes. The paper was due on Monday, but all I could think about was how I'd rather be outside playing tennis now in Kissena Park. Though I had narrowly missed making the Queens College tennis team this year, I had high hopes for my junior year.

Finally, when I realized that I wasn't getting anywhere with the paper, I went downstairs to get something to eat. As I opened the refrigerator door, the clatter of high heels caught my attention. Grabbing an apple, I went into the living room and peered out the window. Gertrude Pinsky was marching down her driveway, a glimmering silver mane fanning over her shoulders and back. Her fierce, protruding eyes saluted mine, as ebullient breasts beckoned through the chartreuse membrane of her blouse. Feeling my ears grow hot, I fled from the window. From the depths of the living room, though, I continued to observe Gertrude, who was standing still now, shaking her fist. "I'll beat the crap out of you, you lousy mutt. Now I have to clean up your filthy goddamn mess," she proclaimed to her huge, cross-eyed dog, Buster, who apparently had relieved himself quite prolifically in the driveway. The culprit appeared remorseful, whimpering as he cowered against the side steps.

Quivering with laughter, I darted out of the living room and hurried upstairs. Recalling Gertrude's inviting look, I imagined her harsh commands initiating me into the mysteries and ecstasies of sex. I saw headlines blaring in that subway rider's opiate, the *New York Daily News*, "19-Year Old Boy And 60-Year Old Woman Discovered Together By Husband, Who Shoots To Death Wife, Then Lover, Outstanding Queens College Student."

Actually, Gertrude was probably only in her midfifties, and her physical appearance was not prepossessing. She was dumpy and double-chinned, her sallow face resembling a choleric frog's. After a brief honeymoon period, there had been one ridiculous skirmish after another between Gertrude and my family, ever since we'd moved next door to her on Parsons Boulevard six years ago. Gertrude intrigued me; her fiery personality somehow set her apart from her blander neighbors. Despite her pugnacious ways, however, Gertrude appeared well-liked on our block. Jews made up slightly over a third of the population on the block, and the Jewish women associated closely with one another. Gertrude was more a part of this semi-suburban neighborhood of detached red brick houses and well-tended lawns than my family was with its alien intellectual and political interests.

Sitting down at my desk, I pictured myself hitting

a succession of crisp crosscourt backhands and withering fore-
hands down the line as Louise Cole watched admiringly.
Louise was a small girl whose lively, sensitive gray eyes seemed
to sparkle with great joy and wisdom. We'd never exchanged
more than a few words in high school and now merely smiled
and nodded when we passed on the Queens College campus.
Still, I nurtured dreams of one day getting up the courage to
begin a serious conversation with Louise. Gawky and pain-
fully shy, I'd had exactly two dates in my two years of college,
both blind ones and total disasters.

Sighing, I began reading *Babbit* by Sinclair Lewis, one of
my literary idols. I was an English major; and so naturally,
another one of my aspirations was to write The Great Ameri-
can Novel. I was aware that my occasional scribblings were
blatant imitations of Sinclair Lewis or Thomas Wolfe, but
figured that at my age they'd probably been imitating some-
one, too. I saw the collected works of Steve Maltz someday
assuming their rightful place beside the writings of Sinclair
Lewis, Thomas Wolfe, Sherwood Anderson, and Theodore
Dreiser.

Feeling restless, I got up and went to the window. Ger-
trude was spraying the front lawn with a hose, one bejewelled
hand arched jauntily on her hip, eyes squinting against the
smoke pouring from cigaret and holder jammed into the
corner of her scarlet mouth. She was wearing rather audacious-
ly revealing pink toreador pants along with her sleeveless
chartreuse blouse. Mr. Levine, the cabinet maker, was across
the street, thick shoulders slumped wearily, as he trudged to-
ward his house down the block. Gertrude's eyes flashed hun-
grily at him as he approached. "How are you, Mr. Levine?"
she inquired, smiling sweetly.

"Oh, I guess I can't complain, Gertrude," he replied.

I wryly observed that Gertrude stood somewhat straight-
er now, the smile clinging to her face for a while afterwards, as
if the brief exchange of greetings represented some special tri-
umph for her.

I continued watching as Gertrude; Mrs. Schecter, who
lived directly across the street; and Mrs. Goldstein, our next

door neighbor, conducted a long distance conversation. Mrs. Schecter was a pale, worn-looking woman with an irritatingly nasal voice and a brood of small, whiny children. Clad in pedal pushers and sweat shirt and sporting a poodle cut, she held a weeder. Mrs. Goldstein, dressed tastefully in dark skirt and white blouse, bleached blonde hair neatly arranged in a bun, was about Gertrude's age. She and her husband, a used car dealer, were the Pinskys' best friends on the block.

"Did you ever see such beautiful weather so early in April?" Mrs. Goldstein was saying.

"It feels like summer already," Mrs. Schecter added.

"With this weather, tell me, who needs Miami?" Gertrude declared, gesturing emphatically.

Then they started talking about Mah Jongg, which apparently all of them played. Laughing at myself for wasting time with this sort of nonsense, I returned to *Babbit*. I'd been reading for some time when I heard the chugging noise of an engine. Going to the window again, I saw Gertrude's husband, Milton, returning from his lumber yard. On Saturdays he worked only half days instead of his usual ten or twelve hours. Carefully maneuvering his station wagon beside Gertrude's shiny gray Cadillac in the garage, Milton wobbled along the driveway, a hairy, bald-headed billiard ball of a man with a soggy cigar stub protruding from thick lips. He spoke in a smothered, guttural voice to Buster, who wagged his tail excitedly and barked.

"Milton, would you do me a favor? The garbage pail is full already. Go bring it to the front of the house," Gertrude called from the kitchen window.

Milton's head bobbed obediently. With waddling, flat-footed steps, he proceeded to lug the garbage pail along the driveway. He seemed to have about as much personality as the cigar stub in his mouth. I was about to return to my book when my parents came home; I went downstairs to help them carry in some groceries.

At supper there was the usual talk of books and politics, C. Wright Mills, the Cuban revolution, the peace movement, Bertrand Russell. My parents were old leftists.

"How is your paper coming, Steve?" my mother inquired as we sipped our coffee.

I hesitated, then shrugged. "Not so hot, I guess."

A concerned expression came onto her broad face. "What's the problem? Would it help to discuss it with your father and me?"

I shook my head. "No thanks, it's all right. I just need to concentrate a little better, that's all."

My father glanced over at me from his dishwashing. He was a large, sallow-faced man whose dark crewcut was faintly speckled with gray. "If you do decide that discussing it would be helpful, though, just let us know," he offered.

My mother's small, narrowed eyes were intent on mine. "That's right, Steve. Don't be ashamed to ask us for help if you need it. After all, your college career is important to us, too. The better you do now, the easier it will be to get into a good graduate school and maybe even get a scholarship, too. You've done quite well so far, and there's no reason why you shouldn't continue doing good work."

"Yeah, all right," I mumbled, getting up to go to my room.

Upstairs I paced back and forth, shaking my head. Apparently, my so-called college career is much more important to my parents than to me, I mused. What if I actually quit school, though, to pursue my dreams, traveling, meeting all sorts of people, getting various jobs, and becoming a real writer? I savored these thoughts for a while, then laughed sardonically. Here I am engaging in pipe-dreams again, I reflected. After all, what entitles me to think I'm special, a potential Thomas Wolfe or Sherwood Anderson? Sighing and with a somewhat guilty conscience, I picked up *Babbit*, promising myself to get to my school work soon.

On Sunday night a few meager ideas on the subject of fruit flies finally visited my brain, and I scribbled away, padding generously. *Science for Liberal Arts Majors* was a required course, and I never expended much energy on required courses. Last term I'd gotten a *B* on a paper for art appreciation in which I'd pretended to discover all sorts of abstruse connections among various Madonna and Child paintings down through the centuries.

On Monday afternoon, coming home from my classes, I observed Gertrude overseeing a young man who was repairing a section of the patio in her back yard. She was frequently overseeing young men puttering with her house or yard, as if that were her vocation in life. Her two-story red brick house, with all the remodeling done to it so far, looked like a wedding cake and stood out from all the other two-story brick houses on the block. That afternoon her protuberant eyes photographed the man's every movement as she hovered over him, issuing a steady stream of instructions. Yet in heels, purple silk blouse, and orange toreador pants, with silver hair cascading over her shoulders, and gleaming, tapered fingernails, she exuded silky charm as well. During a break, she brought the workman a bottle of beer, laughing and chatting with him in a soft, intimate voice. They were an odd pair, Gertrude wrapped in all her finery, like a well-preserved Christmas present, and the workman, thickset and baby-faced, in army fatigues, work shoes, damp tee shirt, and a Brooklyn Dodgers baseball cap.

Sighing, I got a glass of milk and went upstairs to do some homework. My reading of Robert Browning was interrupted about an hour later by the sound of loud voices. Looking out the window, I saw Gertrude pointing disdainfully at the wet gray patch on the patio. "You call that a job?" she demanded. "It won't last two days with all them cracks in it. One little rain will wash it all away."

"But, ma'am, that's the way it's supposed to look until it dries," the man protested.

"Go tell that to some other sucker. It don't look right to me, that's all. I can't pay you until you do it over," Gertrude insisted, pudgy hands jammed onto her hips.

He stared at her, his sturdy, pleasant face wearing a stunned expression. Finally he said, "I get paid by the hour. If you want me to do more work, you'll have to pay me for the extra time."

Gertrude's voice rose sharply. "I will not pay you extra.

You did a lousy job already, and so I shouldn't have to pay you one penny extra. You ruined my patio."

A spasm of nervous laughter escaped the workman. "You gotta be kidding," he said.

She flailed her fist at him. "So you think I'm kidding, you lousy crook? I'll call the police on you. I'll get someone else to do it, and then I'll have to pay him twice as much just to make up for the crummy work you did. Now if you fix it up a little bit, I'll pay you for three hours work, anyway."

Scratching his ear, the workman briefly pondered Gertrude's offer. Meanwhile, people from several nearby houses were craning their necks out of windows, gaping at all this commotion. The workman said, "I can't do that, ma'am. I worked five hours for you so—"

"Take it or leave it!" she hissed.

"I'll have to take you to Small Claims Court, then," he said, shrugging.

"Go ahead, take me to Small Claims Court!" she shrieked. "My neighbors will all testify what kind of crummy work you did. I ask for an honest man, and this is what I get, a crook! Now get out of here, or I'll call the police on you!"

I watched the workman hastily pack up his tools as Gertrude continued to berate him. One or two of the onlookers were silently shaking their heads, but Gertrude seemed oblivious to those of us who'd witnessed the incident. When the workman had left, she stormed inside the house, muttering under her breath. Only Gertrude would have the gall to pull a cheap stunt like that, I thought.

A short while later at the supper table, I was describing the incident to my parents. "If he takes her to court, he'll need some witnesses," my father said, pausing before a forkfull of string beans.

My mother sighed heavily. "I wouldn't be surprised if he just forgets about it and thanks his lucky stars he's rid of her. You know, she always tries to steal my cleaning women since all the agencies must be wise to her by now."

"It's incredible how she keeps on getting away with everything," I remarked, chewing on some meatloaf. "I guess the other *yentas* on the block must think she's real great stuff."

My mother leaned forward, speaking in a low voice. "I'll tell you a little secret, Steve. None of them are exactly crazy about Gertrude, but no one really wants to tangle with her either. I understand that the women in the Mah Jongg club would like to kick Gertrude out."

"I thought they all liked her," I said.

My mother took a sip of tomato juice, then smiled slyly. "Well, they pretend to, anyway. But I've talked to several of them, and they all think she's terribly crude. They seem to feel that Gertrude's crass behavior gives the Jews on the block a bad name, especially Mrs. Schoenfeld, whose husband is a rabbi."

My father shook his head. "What nonsense! As if anyone can tell the difference between the Jews and the non-Jews on this block, or even cares! They all keep their lawns neatly trimmed, cheat in business, and are appallingly ignorant when it comes to knowing what's going on in the world."

"Of course that whole Jewish business is rather silly," my mother agreed. "But what else do these women have to cling to? Their families and their Jewishness. I think what really bothers them the most, though, is that Gertrude's always giving their husbands the eye. I know that lump of a husband of hers doesn't exactly thrill her to death, but still. . . ." My mother paused, then said to me, "I myself have seen Gertrude give your father a look that would make Sadie Thompson look like kids' stuff."

I laughed embarrassedly, and my father turned red. Both my mother and I teased him about Gertrude, which he took in fairly good spirits. Yet there was something forced about our merriment, as if Gertrude were a destructive force of nature that must be stoically endured.

Several days later I got my paper back from Professor Doakes. The old geezer had given me a *C-*, my lowest mark since entering college. At first I silently cursed old Malcolm out. Then I considered dropping out of school, moving down to the Village, asking Louise to drop out, too, and come live with me as I began work on The Great American Novel. But finally, realizing that I was just being silly, I vowed to make a more serious effort for the rest of *Introduction to Science, Part 2.*

When I came home from my classes that afternoon, Gertrude and Mrs. Goldstein were standing practically toe to toe on Mrs. Goldstein's front steps, and Gertrude was screaming, "The hell with your goddamn Mah Jongg club! Who needs it! You all think you're better than me because you got an education and you were born here. Well, I got news for you. Milton and me could buy and sell all of you. You're a bunch of pikers. We give more to the temple than the rest of you put together. And you call yourselves Jews! Feh! You're nothings, just a crummy bunch of nothings!"

"Look, Gertrude," Mrs. Goldstein sputtered, her round face beet red.

"Don't 'look Gertrude' me! I thought you were my friend, and so you go stab me in the back. After all the things I done for you, too. You don't give a good goddamn for nobody or nothing except yourself."

"People in glasses houses shouldn't throw stones," Mrs. Goldstein retorted, as Gertrude dismissed her with a wave of the hand, clattering down the steps and stalking away. Spitting vehemently on the sidewalk and mumbling to herself, she didn't deign to cast a backward glance at Mrs. Goldstein, who just stared after Gertrude, then sighed and went back inside the house.

Wave upon wave of laughter spilled from me. At last someone had found a chink in the old rhino's hide! Then I recoiled from the sound of something thudding against the wall next door and crashing to the floor. The rest of the afternoon was spasmodically punctuated by these jarring noises accompanied by Gertrude's loud swearing. And in the evening her crackling voice, like a whip, lashed out again and again at either Milton or Buster.

To my surprise, the next morning was relatively quiet. In the evening, my mother told me of her conversation with Mrs. Goldstein earlier in the day. "It seems that the incident with the workman was the last straw. It's been making the rounds of the neighborhood, and the women in the Mah Jongg club decided they would just have to tell Gertrude that she wasn't welcome as a member any more. And after they did that, all hell broke loose, of course."

"I didn't believe I'd see the day when someone said no to Gertrude," I said.

"Neither did I," my mother replied. "But let's see what happens. I wouldn't be surprised if she tries to weasel her way back into the Mah Jongg club. The woman might be crazy, but she's also quite shrewd."

The next morning, as I started off to school, I observed several cartons of old, battered lumber in front of the Goldsteins' house. I smiled and shook my head, recalling that Gertrude had done the exact same thing to us several years ago after some petty quarrel. We'd exchanged the cartons with her once or twice, finally capitulating and dumping them in Kissena Park.

My homework that night was interrupted by Gertrude's indignant voice. She was craning her neck out the front window and yelling, "What are you doing, putting that crap on my property? You're trespassing on my property. I'll call the police on you."

The cartons were all in front of her house now; and Mr. Goldstein, as he returned to his own house, retorted, "Go ahead, Gertrude, call the police. It will save us a phone call."

"Pikers! *Hozzarai!*" Gertrude called after his retreating back.

The next morning the cartons were clustered once again in front of the Goldsteins' house. That evening I watched the Goldsteins load the cartons into the trunk of their black Oldsmobile and head down the block toward Kissena Park. Once again, Gertrude had won the war of the cartons, but from the angry look on the Goldsteins' faces, it appeared that Gertrude's maneuver to regain entrance into the Mah Jongg club had not succeeded.

As I left for school the next morning, I observed Gertrude wearing a mink coat and pillbox hat, even though it was early May and quite warm now. She was getting into her glossy gray Cadillac, and I wondered whether she had some high-class assignation as she sped off, the inevitable cigaret dangling from her lips, eyes straight ahead, chin lifted haughtily.

At the supper table, my mother informed me where Gertrude had been. "It must have been some spectacle," she related, shaking her head in amazement. "That woman has enough *hutzpah* for the whole borough of Queens and probably Brooklyn and the Bronx, too. Imagine, she marched right in to Dr. Schecter's dental office, and in front of the receptionist and the patients acted as if she and Dr. Schecter were having some torrid love affair. It was horribly embarrassing, of course, and finally the only way they could get rid of her was to threaten to call the police. Mrs. Schecter was practically in tears this afternoon, but she says that she and the other women are determined not to let Gertrude back into the Mah Jongg club no matter what."

I laughed grimly. "I don't think it's the police they should call," I said.

On Saturday afternoon, I watched as Gertrude's two married daughters, their husbands, and two babies were all out on the ornate front porch, with its white wooden overhang, plastic lawn chairs, and wheeled table covered with drinks and hors d'ouevres. Sheltered from the warm sunlight, one of the men wore natty bermuda shorts and a monogrammed, short-sleeved white polo shirt, as if he'd just come from the golf course. The other son-in-law, with crewcut and horn-rimmed glasses, and pale blue seersucker suit, looked like a successful young executive. The two daughters, plump and matronly, were almost replicas of each other, in bouffant hair-dos and bright dresses, with heavily made-up faces. Gertrude, in a pink dress and heels, her hair done up in a demure bun, clattered about on sausage legs, the gracious hostess plying everyone with food and drink. She spoke in a loud, elated voice, as if she were conducting a television program for the whole block to watch, especially the Mah Jongg club. Now they would see, of course, that they'd cruelly misjudged Gertrude, that she was at heart the family woman *par excellence*.

On Monday afternoon, returning from my classes, I saw

Gertrude out front watering her lawn. Pretending to be deeply absorbed in thought, I tried to slip quickly past her. I was surprised to hear Gertrude clear her throat, then call out pleasantly, "It's a beautiful day, isn't it?"

My vocal chords refused to work so unaccustomed was I to conversing with Gertrude. Finally I said, "Yes, it is."

"You just coming home from school?" she asked.

"Yeah."

"You must be very good in school," she said, sucking greedily on her cigaret holder and flashing me a brilliant smile.

My perspiring body drew in upon itself as I nodded feebly.

"You know, I need someone to do a little light work in my yard. It's very easy. You could do it after school," Gertrude informed me.

I stared at her for a moment, then said quickly, "Thanks, I'm sorry, but I have a lot of school work to do."

Gertrude's dazzling smile persisted. "It won't take you that long, maybe a couple of hours. I'd do it myself except I don't feel so good right now. You'll make a little extra money."

"Thanks, but I really can't," I said, edging away from her.

Gertrude shrugged brusquely, and the smile leaked out of her eyes. "All right, I'll get someone else," she snapped, turning away.

Relieved, I hurried into my house. Laughter poured from me as I related the incident to my mother.

"She's lonely," my mother said. "The woman has hardly said boo to me for the past two years, and now she's suddenly coming over to visit and acting as if she's my dearest friend. She talked to me for almost two hours about her daughters and grandchildren and about what shits the Jewish women on the block are. She's been making an effort to cultivate the non-Jews on the block. I think she's decided to show the Mah Jongg club that she can live without them."

That night I had an unsettling dream. Somehow Gertrude had managed to lure me into her house, and we were in bed together with our clothes off. In the midst of our lovemaking, which Gertrude had carefully supervised, she suddenly started shouting that I was a young, bumbling fool and that I should get out of her bed. Frantically throwing on my clothes, I stumbled out of her house. Coming out of my dream, I woke up trembling and plastered with sweat.

Then I got absorbed in my own affairs for a while, forgetting about Gertrude. I was busy finishing up papers for several classes and preparing for my finals. Also I saw Louise that week. As I glimpsed the brisk, slightly pigeon-toed walk which I knew by heart, a tremor of anticipation ran through me. Louise was approaching me outside Jefferson Hall, the English building. This time I really have to talk to her, I told myself, despite wobbly knees. To my chagrin, my exuberant "hi" came out sounding like a grotesque croak. Still, Louise graciously returned my greeting, her marvelous gray eyes regarding me warmly. I wracked my brain for something clever to say, but by the time I came up with something, Louise was at least 20 yards away, receding into a cluster of other students. There was a dull ache in my chest as I stood staring after her, as if my ankles were bound by chains. Suddenly I realized that I would never talk to Louise, that she was more satisfying to me this way, as a vision that could visit me day or night, whenever I summoned it.

In the next two weeks or so, I studied diligently, polishing off my term papers and finishing up my finals. The afternoon I returned from my last final my mother said to me, "Have you noticed, Steve? No one has watered the lawn or cut the grass at the Pinskys' for the past several weeks now."

Taking a swallow of milk, I glanced out the window. The Pinskys' usually trim, bright-green lawn was an unkempt shade of brown. "I haven't seen her around lately," I commented.

"I have no great love for Gertrude, believe me, but I'm worried about her," my mother confided. "For the past week or so I think she's just been sitting in the house, drinking and watching the soap operas. I don't even think she feeds the dog much any more."

Now that my finals were over, I intermittently kept watch over Gertrude's driveway, and my vigilance was eventually rewarded. The next afternoon I glimpsed Gertrude setting out

food for Buster in the driveway, probably because of his in-
sistent howling. The dog attacked the food as if he hadn't
eaten for days, and Gertrude swore at him under her breath.
She was in floppy slippers and a blue bathrobe; her hair was
short and rumpled, her bulbous eyes puffy and red-rimmed.
I gaped at her, as if at some monstrous apparition. She caught
me staring at her and shot me a furious glance. Shamefaced,
I backed away from the window, feeling like a peeping Tom.
Unexpectedly, I found myself feeling sorry for Gertrude.
Like me, she was a dreamer, but reality had treated her
dreams more harshly than mine. For a moment, I even felt
myself rooting for Gertrude to be taken back into the bosom
of the Mah Jongg club and indulged in her mad fantasies that
she was an enchanting and beautiful young woman.

Well, there isn't much left to relate of this semi-suburban
melodrama. I received a final grade of B in Professor Doakes'
course and A's and B's in my other courses. That summer I
was a recreation worker in a playground in central Flushing.
The job kept me quite busy, and I didn't give the Pinskys
much thought, until one sluggish afternoon in late June.
Lounging about on a day off, I encountered Gertrude outside
watering her front lawn. She was dressed in her old flamboy-
ant manner, and I turned hastily away from the unmistakable
wink she directed at me. As I headed in the opposite direction
from Gertrude, I wondered whether my imagination was play-
ing tricks on me or whether now Gertrude had attained a new
level of maturity, a hard-earned serenity and acceptance of
life's tragic aspect.

Later that afternoon, while my mother was waiting for
her next remedial reading pupil to arrive, I remarked, "I'm
surprised, but it looks like Gertrude has finally gotten over
that whole business with the Mah Jongg club."

My mother smiled broadly. "I didn't ever tell you what
happened, did I? Well, get a load of this. Apparently, Ger-
trude found that her aggressive tactics didn't work so she de-
cided to change her approach and play on the other women's
sympathies. Evidently, she sounded so pathetic on the phone
that she had them all convinced she was on the verge of a

nervous breakdown and suicide, all because of their rejection of her, of course. And so, feeling guilty as hell, they relented and decided to let Gertrude back into the Mah Jongg club."

I shook my head in amazement. "That's incredible, it really is."

"I told you that woman was no dumbbell. In fact, I'd say that given half an opportunity, she'd con the pants off the devil himself," my mother replied.

I was about to agree when the bell rang, and my mother went to open the door for her pupil. I sat for a long time in the dining room, musing bleakly about Gertrude and the human weakness she knew how to manipulate so well. Despite all the idealism I'd been raised on, it made me wonder whether there was really much hope for any of us. Still, I couldn't help feeling a certain perverse admiration for Gertrude, who never relented in the pursuit of her tawdry little dreams. Finally, I got up to change into my tennis clothes. If Gertrude, after being bounced from the Mah Jongg club, could rise from the dead, like Lazarus, then the very least I can do is make the Queens College tennis team next year, I decided.

THE PLAYGROUND

IN THE SUMMER OF 1959, after my sophomore year at Queens College, I was a recreation worker in a playground in central Flushing. On a warm, sluggish morning in early June, my first day, Al Martinelli, the maintenance man, was showing me around. The playground was a large concrete area of one square block surrounded by a thick gray fence. Near the 41st Avenue entrance was a small, square, brick park house looking like an ancient fortress. Near the park house were some scarred, faded green benches, a stone table with a checkerboard stamped on it, a knock hockey table, sandbox, wading pool, and a flag pole with the stars and stripes fluttering lazily from the apex. Further away were two weathered-looking slides, some swings, a jungle gym, a faded softball diamond, a basketball court with two rusty, battered hoops and backboards, and two back-to-back handball courts enclosed by a fence. Our inspection proceeded smoothly until we discovered that one of the swings had been flung on top of the over-

"Gee, don't you feel excited, Francesca? Now we'll be listed in Ripley's *Belive It Or Not.* We could even sell them to the zoo and make a lot of money."

She wasn't amused. "I know this is all very trying, Elliot, but please be patient. I'll call the Dog and Cat Hospital the first thing in the morning."

"But supposing they get ravenous in the middle of the night? I'm not volunteering my delicious flesh to two hunger crazed felines. No, we have to do something tonight."

"Well, what would you suggest?"

He hesitated. "We might . . . I think we might have to take them to . . . well, to the Humane Society. . . . Maybe someone will want them. You never know in a place like Berkeley."

"And if no one does want them?"

He shrugged. "Then I guess they'll just have to be put to sleep."

She gazed at him in horror. "They're my babies, Elliot. How can you talk so calmly about killing them?"

He laughed. "Babies did you say? They're monsters now. We'll both have to become executives to afford them. That'll be the end of my writing and your painting. That's what I call real murder. . . . But you know something? I'm really beginning to think they won't come back."

"Don't you wish! Well, they're still my cats, Elliot, even if they do look rather odd now. So if they go, I go, too." Tears dripped down her quivering cheeks.

He examined her taut face, then said, "Look, I'm sorry. I don't really want anything to happen to them. It's just that it's all so bizarre."

She nodded, brushing away tears. He stroked her hair, then kissed her. She smiled. They were sitting on the couch being quietly affectionate when Serious strode in from the balcony and headed toward them. Francesca petted the cat, who nuzzled her head against Francesca's hand. "See, she's just the same as ever, our same old lovable Serious."

"Yeah, I guess they were just hungry before, that's all."

Serious pushed her head into Elliot's shoulder. He began to fondle her. She made her usual goo-goo eyes at him, then leaped into his lap. Gritting his teeth, he spread his legs, bracing himself to hold her. She produced soft, voluptuous growls as he caressed her broad back and neck. Then she rolled over, exposing her snowy belly, as she squirmed about in her old provocative way. Despite the pressure on his legs and the effort to keep Serious from tumbling off his lap, Elliot was beginning to enjoy playing with her. "Gee, you know, actually she looks pretty good now, kind of like a panther or mountain lion," he observed.

Francesca laughed and threw her arms around Elliot, kissing him. "You're a softie at heart, Elliot. I knew Serious would woo you back eventually. She hasn't lost one bit of her charm, that's for sure."

"You know, maybe we should start looking for a bigger place," he suggested. "They can't be very comfortable in a small apartment like this. Actually, we should probably look for a place out in the country."

Francesca kissed him again. "I love you, Elliot," she exclaimed. "You really do understand my needs, don't you?"

Elliot was about to reply when Silly thundered into the living room. Serious immediately sprang off Elliot's lap, growling at her son. The cats began warily circling each other, hissing, roaring, spitting, and grimacing. The fur stood up stiffly on their backs and necks, and their elongated tails slid ominously from side to side. Then, like a whirlwind, Serious and Silly were furiously chasing one another about the living room, loudly toppling chairs, tables, and various other objects.

"Oh, Jesus, there goes my novel!" Elliot moaned, as his carefully typed pages flew in all directions. Several times he and Francesca barely managed to get out of the path of an onrushing cat. Only an occasional glancing blow was struck in the melee, however. The main damage seemed to be to the living room and Elliot and Francesca's nerves. Finally the two antagonists stood panting, glowering at each other across a sea of litter, but making no attempt to resume their battle. A strong, noxious odor pervaded the room now.

Francesca remarked grimly, "Silly must have sprayed during their fight. The living room will be absolutely uninhabitable unless we find some way to eliminate the stench."

He sighed, nodding morosely.

Then the cats demanded more food. "I'll take care of it, Elliot. Meanwhile, maybe you could pick up a little around the living room," Francesca suggested.

Slowly, without enthusiasm, Elliot began trying to restore some semblance of order. After a short while, he wearily gave up. Francesca, lips pursed sternly, was setting out slabs of leftover meatloaf, six raw eggs, two bowlsful of cottage cheese, two of yogurt, and several large chunks of cheddar cheese. Within minutes, it had all vanished. The cats licked their chops, as they usually did after an especially good meal, then diligently proceeded to wash themselves. They settled down in opposite cornears of the room, Serious on top of several pages of Elliot's novel, and Silly perched on two of Francesca's sketchpads. Their large, round eyes slowly fluttered shut.

"Maybe we'll have some peace now for a little while," Elliot said. "I guess I didn't do too great a job cleaning up the living room."

"Don't worry about it. I don't have the energy to even think about that right now."

"Yeah, you said it! Say, would you like some brandy?"

She smiled. "Any more stupid questions?"

They went into the bedroom, closed the door, and started belting down brandy. Francesca was shaking her head, declaring sadly that it looked as if they would have to give the cats up. Tears quivered on her eyelashes, and Elliot felt sorry for her. He ran his hand slowly over Francesca's thigh.

"Please, Elliot, not tonight," she said, pulling away from him.

Silently they drank some more brandy, and soon Francesca began yawning strenuously. She kissed Elliot and murmured a drowsy goodnight. Her eyes slid shut, as her head sank to the pillow. Anticipating a long and sleepless night, he gulped down the rest of the brandy. The warmth spread quickly through him, and soon he was able to fall asleep, too. During the night, though, he thought he heard loud, thudding noises accompanied by indignant howls, as if the cats were hurling themselves against the bedroom door.

The next morning Elliot and Francesca woke up about a quarter to nine. "They've probably taken the rest of the house apart by now," he growled, his throat fuzzy, his head dull from brandy.

Cautiously he opened the bedroom door. He started back, stunned. Serious and Silly were reclining on their forepaws in the hallway; they were extraordinarily small, like ordinary cats. Their purrs were soft and delicate. Elliot laughed, infinitely relieved, amused by their littleness. "Jesus, this is really weird," he said, rubbing his sleep-filled eyes to make sure they weren't deceiving him.

"Isn't it?" Francesca agreed.

"Anyway, now things should be back to normal once we straighten up the mess in the living room," he said.

Francesca fondled and hugged Silly as if she hadn't seen him for months. "My little Silly, I'm so glad you look like a normal cat again. Now I don't have to worry any more about giving you up, baby boy."

Serious' claws on Elliot's pajama leg felt ridiculously light. He ruffled the fur on her small, sleek head, playing with her like a toy.

Francesca called the Berkeley Dog and Cat Hospital from the bedroom. She argued with the receptionist for a while, finally persuading her to put Dr. Schwartzkopf on the line. Francesca excitedly explained the situation to the vet and then listened, occasionally nodding or exclaiming in surprise. Elliot watched Francesca intently, but it was hard to guess what the vet was actually saying. Then Francesca thanked Dr. Schwartzkopf and hung up.

"He said they've actually had a few cases like this before, and that it's probably a rare cat disease called the twelve hour virus," she informed Elliot.

He laughed. "The twelve hour virus?"

"Yes. They think it might have something to do with a low resistance to negative ions. Something happens to the growth hormones for twelve hours, and then all of a sudden they go back to normal. It's a whole new field of feline pathology they're just beginning to explore."

Elliot shook his head in amazement. "Boy, the things they come up with! Well, at least it's over with now. Except they probably want to examine the cats."

"Yes, they'd like to see them as soon as possible."

"Anyway, I'll make some coffee now."

He headed for the kitchen. At the end of the hallway, he stopped and stared. The living room was in perfect order, just exactly as it had been when they'd returned home yesterday evening. Elliot blinked repeatedly, but everything remained decidedly normal-looking. He sniffed; the oppressive odor was gone, too. He gazed quizzically at the tiny, furry creatures scurrying about his tidy living room.

"Hey, Francesca, hurry up, come over here! Take a look at this!" Elliot called, wondering whether he was going crazy.

THE SECOND AMERICAN REVOLUTION

AFTER WORKING FOR YEARS to elevate the consciousness of the American public, the *Fat Is Fabulous* movement had finally become the dominant force in American life. They had recently elected as president of the country, Earl (Mountain) Tubbs, a country western singer, whose chief campaign slogan was, "I'm 300 pounds, and I'm proud of every sweet, juicy ounce of it." The new vice-president, Virginia (Butterball) Biggs, a 250 pound ex-construction worker, had often used the phrase, "Sure, I'm fat, but you're nuts if you think I'm going to nibble lettuce and cottage cheese." The *Fat Is Fabulous* movement had also captured overwhelming control of the Senate and House of Representatives. Of the 100 members of the Senate, 26 tipped the scales at 300 pounds or over, and 41 of their colleagues ranged between 250 and 300 pounds.

Escargot Hemingway, till recently one of the top

fashion models in America, stabbed fingernails in the air
like blood-red daggers as she stalked the Persian rug in
the inner sanctum of Pierre Au Courant, one of the lead-
ing fashion designers in America. "It's ridiculous," she
shouted, her gaunt, elegantly sculpted face tinged with
pain. "I haven't worked in over two months now for
heaven's sake, and yet I can model circles around every
single one of those fat, frumpy monstrosities who've
been getting all the jobs lately. Christ, I've starved my-
self for years to get where I am. I'm tired of surfing and
water skiing and snorkeling and improving my sun tan.
I want to work."

Au Courant threw up his hands and sighed lightly.
"Naturally, my dear Escargot, I happen to agree with
you about the, let us say, ludicrous aspects of the situ-
ation, but there is nothing, absolutely nothing I can do
about it. For one thing, the fashions have all been changed,
actually, revolutionized, and a svelte-looking woman like
you would appear completely absurd in them. There-
fore. . . ."

"Let's go back to the old fashions, then," Escargot
said.

Au Courant's pale, well-bred face looked infinitely
sad as he glanced at the desk he was sitting at. Arranged
on it in neat piles were several different versions of the
sack dress, Au Courant's current fashion sensation. "That
would be impossible, my dear. If I tried something like
that, I would be out on my ear in no time," he explained.
"Face it, Escargot. Times have changed. Apparently,
women are tired of the tyranny of being thin. They want
to eat whatever they want; they're tired of all that exer-
cise; they want to let their stomachs out, to wear loose,
comfortable clothes modeled by fat women, women they
can identify with."

"Bullshit!" she retorted. "It's just a phase, like that
punk thing. Everyone's become jaded, so this is some
new kind of kick, I suppose. But how long can this idiocy
last? Men will get tired of cows masquerading as women.

If just one designer, like you, for instance, Pierre, started to buck this stupid trend, then another one would and another one, and then. . . ."

Pierre slowly shook his head. "I'm afraid it's not that simple. Take a good look around you. The fat people, they control everything now in America, not just the fashions. It's all been turned topsy turvy. And in Europe, too, France, Italy, England, Sweden, they are very close to taking over. So unless you're fat, Escargot, I'm sorry but I can't help you. I think you ought to consider—"

"Oh go to hell, you ballless faggot!" Escargot screamed. "Just because you've gained 70 pounds and shaved your head and wear wrinkled clothes doesn't mean that I have to destroy myself. I think you're vile and despicable-looking. Where's your pride? Once your fashions were the best in the world, and I helped you make them the best. Now you make shit, and you treat me like a nothing. I hate you, Au Courant!"

Looking like a tired, rumpled Buddha, Au Courant didn't say anything. He reached into the pocket of his tan chinos, withdrawing a seeded roll, which he began gnawing on urgently. She glared at him a moment longer, then stamped toward the door. Flinging it open, she strode past Au Courant's secretary, a huge woman exuberantly wolfing down chocolate cake, who was dressed in baggy blue jeans, tennis shoes, and a tee shirt proclaiming: Fat Is Fun. The secretary met Escargot's glowering gaze with a disdainful look of her own. Adorning one wall was a large photograph of Au Courant's current top fashion model, Mary Smith, with the caption: The More The Merrier. Mary was posed in a sack bathing suit, and Escargot went red with anger as she stared at the model's enormous thighs, which reminded her of watermelons. "Gross, gross, gross beyond belief!" Escargot snarled, slamming the door behind her.

She stalked along the hallway, keeping her head in the air so she wouldn't have to see any more of those so-called fabulous fat people who were taking the bread from her mouth. Her eyes were clamped shut as she rode down in the crowded elevator, feeling hemmed in by mounds of intrusive flesh.

When she was finally outside in the warm, humid sunshine, she breathed a sigh of relief. Allowing herself to glance once again at people, she was pained by what she witnessed. Basically, people ignored her, which was so different from the recent past, when she felt everyone looked at her all the time, men with transparent awe and lust burning in their eyes, women with admiration and envy. Then it was a question of never having enough privacy. Now, when they did deign to glance at her, people's expressions usually seemed pitying, as if she were some sort of freak, a dinosaur from an earlier era. In turn, most of the people on the street appeared to Escargot so unphotogenically bulky, dressed so drably in shapeless, muted clothes that she could hardly bear to look at them. When she did occasionally come across a genuinely thin man or woman, they usually slunk along the sidewalk, averting their gaze from hers, as if even making eye contact were a conspiratorial act. Children sometimes laughed or pointed rudely as they passed Escargot, and one or two even tried to touch her, grabbing at her Au Courant black satin culottes, her ruffled organdy blouse. "What's the matter with that lady, mommy?" one of them asked. "Is she sick?"

"She's skinny, dear," her mother patiently explained. "Skinny people have a lot of problems, and they do get sick a lot because they don't know how to take care of themselves."

When Escargot turned her eyes skyward, the billboards offered no solace. Instead of some lithe, tanned woman stretched out languorously beside a glass of milk or bottle of sun tan lotion, there was a paunchy, balding man with horn-rimmed glasses shoving a forkful of spaghetti into his mouth. Above him was the caption: Eat Your Way To Corpulence And Contentment With High-Calorie Big Boy Spaghetti. Escargot felt like screaming.

She waved and shouted for a taxi. The cab started toward her, and she waited for it eagerly, anticipating a relaxed ride home, leaning back and closing her eyes to the outside world, to the nightmare it had become. But as the taxi drew to the curb, an obese eldery woman using a cane stepped past her and reached for the door handle. "I beg your pardon. I was here first," Escargot informed her.

"Insolent bag of bones!" the woman hissed.

She opened the door. "Driver, I signalled for the taxi first, didn't I?" she insisted.

"Of course you did. No doubt about it," he replied.

"You're both liars. I'm calling a policeman," Escargot said.

"Go right ahead, you little twit. See if I care," the woman said, brandishing her cane. Startled, Escargot backed away from her.

"These skinny people, they're all alike, they think the world owes them a living because they're nobler and more deprived than everyone else. Well, I say, if they still insist on being masochistic, then that's their problem," the old woman remarked to the portly driver, who nodded and laughed. She clambered onto the back seat and slammed the door; the taxi quickly started away. Escargot stood there crimson-faced, shaking her fist and shouting curses after the departing vehicle.

Determined to fight harder for her rights the next time, she signalled for another cab. A corpulent man in a three-piece suit who carried an attache case tried to push past her, but Escargot was prepared. Her high-heeled shoe ground down ruthlessly into his foot, causing him to howl in pain and drop his attache case. Not wasting a moment, she found herself sitting triumphantly alone in the back seat of the moving taxi. The driver was on the emaciated side, with prominent cheekbones and a sharp chin, so Escargot eagerly struck up a conversation with him.

"Of course I remember you," he said. "You're

Escargot Hemingway. Man, I was really hot for you
once. I used to dream about going out on a date with
you. You know, I used to buy all those silly women's
magazines just to look at the pictures of you. Wow!
Like I used to have these fantasies that you'd be my
fare someday, and we'd really hit if off, you know."

Escargot giggled happily. "I was beginning to think
everyone had forgotten. Now I'm beginning to feel like
a woman again. Actually, you're the first human being
I've met all day, a man who knows how to appreciate a
thin, glamorous woman." After a pause, she said impul-
sively, "When you're finished for the day, why don't
you stop by my place for a drink."

"Well, thanks. I don't know, though," he began
hesitantly.

"What's the matter?" she demanded. "Aren't I good
enough for you? I don't extend an invitation like that to
just anyone, you know. If you want to be rude. . . ."

"It's not that, Escargot," he said apologetically.
"I'd really love to. It's just that, like things are so weird
these days. You see, I'm trying to change my whole
image. Business is really down for me, you know, be-
cause I'm a real skinny guy. I've actually had people
get out of the cab after they got a good look at me. For
crying out loud, they act like I'm a goddamn leper or
something. What does my weight have to do with driv-
ing a cab?"

"A lot of people seem to be quite prejudiced these
days. I think it's just a phase, though," she said. "It
better be. I'm not ready to retire yet. Christ, I haven't
had any work at all in the past two months."

The driver sighed. "You know, it's gotten so bad
I've made an appointment with a surgeon. A lot of skinny
people are doing that now. You see, I'm a nervous type;
I can eat all day, and still I don't gain any weight. In the
past month I don't know how many milk shakes and hot
fudge sundaes and peanut butter and jelly sandwiches
I've fed my face with. And would you believe it? I

gained maybe half a pound or something. So this doc's
gonna perform an operation on me to slow down my
metabolism. Then I figure I won't have any more of
these hassles. Like I'll be just as fat as the next guy,
then."

"I'll never do anything like that!" Escargot vowed.
"I'd rather kill myself first. The last time I was fat was
when I was 13 years old. I was ugly and unpopular and
so miserable that I cried all the time. So I starved myself
until I became really thin, till I had those gorgeous hollows
in my cheeks and my ribs all stuck out. I felt like a French
film star. Then all the boys began chasing me, and I
couldn't get them to leave me alone. I'm not complain-
ing, of course. My life has been just wonderful. . . . But
then this absurd *Fat Is Fabulous* movement. . . ."

The cabbie grimly shook his head. "I don't know
about you, Escargot, but I can't take it any more. I haven't
even been able to get a date lately. Me, a guy who used
to be pretty popular with the chicks, and now none of
them will even speak to me because they think I look
weird. It's gotten to the point where I don't care how
much weight I gain. Hell, maybe I'll end up looking
like King Farouk or something." He laughed sardoni-
cally.

"Oh, how horrible!" Escargot exclaimed, bursting
into tears. She sobbed the rest of the way home, oblivi-
ous to the fact that her makeup was being smeared.
When the cab pulled up in front of her luxury apartment,
she paid the driver quickly and hurried away. She nod-
ded coolly to the silver-haired doorman, whose previously
lean frame had conspicuously filled out in recent weeks.

In her apartment, Escargot paced back and forth
over a lambskin rug, then made herself a Black Russian.
She turned on the television set but soon shut it with an
angry click. "What an aesthetic wasteland T.V. has be-
come!" she lamented. The thin people on the soap operas
had been replaced by fat ones. The once slender, boyish-
ly handsome doctor now resembled a burly bear, Escargot

felt. And his previously sylphlike mistress inclined unmistakably toward the rotund.

Escargot proceeded to call various friends of hers, all thin people, of course. The news she received wasn't encouraging. Sick Dagger, an eminent rock musician, had decided to emigrate to Communist China, where he felt an ectomorph still had a chance because of the spartan standard of living that prevailed there. Similarly, other lean celebrities had chosen to depart for various countries in Africa, Asia, and Latin America, where most of the population was still thin due to difficult economic conditions. On the other hand, Sarah Saucy Yum Yum, the ravishing model and film star, like the cab driver had opted for surgery. She had been given a long-term movie contract on the condition that she gain at least 75 pounds in the next two months and maintain her lofty numbers for the duration of the contract. And Sheer Bone, the noted singer, dancer, comedienne, and femme fatale, had decided to retire from the entertainment business and devote herself exclusively to domestic life, namely her three children and fourth husband.

Escargot was in a mood of near despair; she pondered killing herself. She refused to emigrate to what she considered a third-rate country, and she didn't want to undergo surgery that would tamper with her body. As she was only 25 years old, she felt retirement was premature. So what else is there left? she wondered.

To make matters worse, in the evening, she received a disheartening phone call from her boyfriend, Darrel Wetsuit, the billionaire entrepreneur. "I can't fight them any longer, Escargot," he moaned. "They'll break me down to a pauper if I keep making wet suits for thin people. So I've decided to make wet suits for fat people. That means I'll have to alter my entire image, of course. I have an appointment with a metabolic surgeon for tomorrow morning. Look, I can arrange one for you, too, Escargot darling. It's a very simple operation; there shouldn't be any complications. Everyone's doing it now."

"No, Darrel," she said firmly. "I'll never do any-
thing so gross. It's against the laws of nature to tamper
with your body like that. No, definitely not."

There was a long pause. Then Darrel said, "I'm
afraid I won't be able to see you any more, Escargot.
You know how it is."

She slammed down the phone and began crying
furiously. Even him, she fumed. Even Darrel. He was
the one person I thought would never give in. Well, good
riddance. He's not worthy of my little finger. Let him
keep his billions!

A short while later she arose from her purple velvet
couch, deciding that she would be brave and principled,
ending her life with an overdose of sleeping pills. On the
way to the bathroom, she wept some more, feeling very
sorry for herself. I'm a martyr to the cause of thinness,
she thought. The only one who's willing to take a stand.
Oh, but it's so unfair. I'm still so young; there are so
many things I haven't tried yet. I should have gotten
into acting and shown people I really have some talent.

As she stood in the bathroom about to open the pill
bottle, she realized that her hands were trembling violent-
ly. She took several deep breaths and closed her eyes,
finally managing to control the shaking. Then she became
aware of fierce rumblings and palpitations emanating from
her stomach. My God! I haven't had anything to eat all
day, except for some black coffee and a hard boiled egg,
she thought. No wonder I lack the energy to kill myself!
A little bit of food in my stomach will make it much eas-
ier. Some of that camembert cheese with a sesame wafer
or two would be divine right now.

She cut two slabs of cheese, put them on crackers
and promptly devoured these morsels. Oh, that tasted
simply marvelous. Two more and that's it, she vowed.
Again the food disappeared rapidly. I'm absolutely fam-
ished, she reflected. I can't remember when I've last felt
this hungry. Two more, though, and that's definitely the
limit. Her famed willpower appeared to have deserted

her, however, and soon she had finished the whole pack-
age of cheese as well as most of the crackers. Oh, my
God, what have I done? she lamented. I've probably
gained at least a couple of pounds already. I can't afford
to look heavy when I kill myself. I must stop right now.

But her stomach still growled, insisting that she con-
tinue appeasing it. With a profound sigh, berating her-
self repeatedly for being a bottomless pit, she selected
some beluga caviar and several slices of Bavarian pumper-
nickel. Within minutes, she had polished off these tasty
viands, and her stomach began feeling warm and mellow.
Her body tingled and purred as if she had swallowed a
magic potion. I'd forgotten how much fun it is to pig
out, she thought. I feel very wicked, like when I used to
eat all that ice cream and cake in secret, afraid my parents
would find out. I owe it to myself to have one genuine
pig-out before I take those pills. I'm skinny so I can
afford to gain a few extra pounds.

She proceeded to put away three containers of
French yogurt, two bananas, and an orange, washing it
all down with two bottles of Perrier water. That French
yogurt is obscenely good, she reflected, gently massaging
her stomach. I wish I'd bought some more of it. Any-
way, I can't kill myself tonight on a full stomach. I'll
just have to wait until tomorrow.

She changed into a loose, comfortable nightgown,
then searched the nearly empty refrigerator and cup-
boards. Pondering for several moments, she went to the
phone and ordered a large mushroom and pepperoni
pizza, a Crab Louie salad, and some chocolate eclairs.
While she waited for her food, she waltzed dreamily
about the apartment, singing softly, savoring the full,
warm sensation that pervaded her whole body. When
the food came, she tore into it as if she hadn't seen any
for days; and after she had disposed of it all, she burped,
then fell contentedly asleep on the purple velvet couch.

When she woke up in the morning, she decided it
was absurd to kill herself. Instead, she ordered a break-

fast of eggs Benedict; bagels, cream cheese, and lox; croissants and jam; and cappuccino. After breakfast she dozed, daydreaming of what she would have for lunch.

Ten days later, Escargot was still eating heartily. She had gained over 50 pounds during this time and was in the habit of pinching herself about the midriff, enjoying the sensuous slide of flesh under her caressing fingertips. She weighed herself at least five times a day, elated at each new climb of the dial. And once or twice a day, she danced naked in front of a large mirror, kneading, stroking, admiring her full, resurrected body. What a fool I was! she occasionally chided herself. I must really have looked like a walking skeleton. Now at least I have some meat on my bones.

She called Au Courant, who told her he would probably be able to use her if she gained another 15 pounds or so. She laughed and said that was easily attainable, requiring only a few more days of normal eating. There was a big smile on Escargot's full face as she hung up the phone. It will feel good to be working again, to be part of things, she thought, letting out her belt another notch, then deciding that some gazpacho salad, along with a few slices of Quiche Lorraine, onion rolls and brie cheese, and a double order of chocolate mousse would really hit the spot for lunch.

head bar. Al scratched hard at his gray crewcut, his lined,
swarthy face turning red. "The wise bastards!" he hissed.
"I'd like to wring every one of their rotten necks."

"Who are they?" I asked.

He waved disgustedly. "Ah, just a bunch of punks, you
know, some smart-alecky teenagers who like to bust my balls.
Their leader is a 17-year old wise guy called Butch O'Leary
who walks with a limp and has just about the foulest mouth
around."

Al stalked inside the park house and returned carrying a
ladder, which he planted underneath the tangled swing. I
watched his short, thick frame in its olive-green uniform mount
the ladder as if it were a gallows. He stood just beneath the top
rung, sighing and sweating as he tugged at and manipulated the
recalcitrant swing. I was apprehensive that he might fall; but
finally, after ten minutes or so, the swing fell free to its nor-
mal position. Rivulets of sweat trickled down Al's brown,
leathery cheeks as he descended the ladder.

"Jeez, it's really hot out here!" he exclaimed, mopping
his large face with a handkerchief. "Now if they know what's
good for them, they'll keep their lousy hands off that swing.
Come on, we might as well go inside and relax for a while."

Both of us drank generously from the water fountain out-
side the men's bathroom before entering the park hut, which
was cavelike and had an air of emptiness, though Al's mainte-
nance tools, some recreation equipment, and a few pieces of
furniture were scattered about. We sat on metal folding chairs
at an old, worn-looking wooden table, and Al lit a cigaret,
letting the smoke drift evenly from his nostrils. His dark,
prominent eyes were red-rimmed, and there was a faint layer
of gray stubble shadowing his jaws.

"This seems like a pretty tough place to work," I said.

Al shrugged. "I've been here eight years, Steve, and I
like most of the kids and older people who come around. It's
mainly just a small bunch you have to keep an eye on. But if
you get after the wise guys right from the start, that'll make
the job easier for both of us. Like the sign says, the rules for
inside the playground are no drinking, no drugs, no gambling,

no hardball playing, and no bike riding. As soon as you see any of them playing cards, tell 'em to break it up right away."

"Even if they're not playing for money?"

Al peered at me as if I were a child. "Look, if they're playing cards you know there's gotta be money involved, and technically that's gambling. It don't look too good, you know, if the foreman happens to see it, and besides, they're usually drinking and swearing, too, and that sets a bad example for the younger kids."

I nodded, trying to match Al's earnest look.

"And another thing," he went on, gazing at me intently. "Don't ever let anyone who isn't a park employee inside the park house, I don't care what they tell you!" He thumped on the table for emphasis. "Let 'em wait outside for their equipment. And that goes double for the girls. If the recreation supervisor or the maintenance foreman ever catches you with a girl inside the park house, they'll fire your ass right on the spot, even if you weren't doing nothing and never intended to and swore it on a stack of Bibles. The point is, you always gotta consider what the public might be thinking since you're a city employee now. And some of these girls here don't got much respect for themselves, y'know what I mean? So you gotta be extra careful." Al took one or two quick puffs on his cigaret, then carefully stubbed it out.

"Yeah, I can see that," I murmured, though curious about those girls.

"Anyway, there's a police call box right outside on the corner of 41st and Bowne." He pointed. "So don't be afraid to use it if someone's giving you a hard time."

I sighed furtively, feeling more like a policeman right now than a recreation worker. We sat for a while in silence as I wondered whether I would last the whole summer in this place, or even a few weeks.

Then Al yawned and glanced at the clock on the wall. "Ten minutes after eleven," he announced. "Lunch is at twelve so I might as well get a little work done before then. I always like to keep on top of the situation. My philosophy is, do your work first, then take it easy afterwards."

I watched him trudge out of the park house, a determined look on his face, as if he'd just been sent out on some vital mission. He was lugging his dustpan and big pushbroom and whistling softly to himself. Near the jungle gym and slides, he began sweeping with smooth, methodical strokes of the broom. I sat back down again, fantasizing that I was playing tennis now or home reading a book. I felt a little better, though, when I began examining the various games and pieces of athletic equipment stacked in a corner that it would be my job to give out. I enjoyed sports and hoped to encounter some kids in the playground who also liked playing ball.

At twelve o'clock, Al and I ate our lunches at the wooden table inside the park house. I gratefully accepted Al's offer of some cold milk from his thermos. Donning black-framed reading glasses, he perused the *Daily News* and absently munched on a cheese sandwich. I chewed my egg salad sandwich and thought about reading my book of Chekhov short stories tomorrow evening when I'd be here by myself. Occasionally, Al looked up from his newspaper to summarize some particularly perverted or grisly story for me. His face mirrored his despairing words as he commented, "You know, people don't seem to care what they do any more. Back when I was a kid, our parents at least tried to teach us some morals and some respect, and I did the same with my kids. Honest to Pete, my parents would have smacked the piss out of me if I'd tried to do one-tenth of what some of these kids do nowadays."

"Do you ever think of getting a different kind of job?" I asked.

Al looked surprised. "What for? This job isn't too bad once you learn the ropes. Before this, me and my wife owned a candy store, and that was ten times worse, believe me. Six days a week from early in the morning to ten o'clock at night at least one of us had to be in that darn candy store. Here, I got the weekends off, and when I go home at five o'clock I'm a free man till the next day, anyway." His eyes traveled to the clock. "Jeez, I got to yakking and forgot all about the time. Lunch was over ten minutes ago." Smiling sheepishly, he yawned and stretched, then folded his newspaper and stood up.

In the afternoon the playground became somewhat busier,
and Al introduced me to a few younger kids. I gave out a check-
er set and some knock hockey equipment, at first just observing,
then after a while playing myself. My spirits were lifted because
finally I had something to do. A chill went through me, how-
ever , when later that afternoon I realized that the hoods were
in the playground. A bunch of them, boys and a few girls,
were bent over a card game spread out on a bench near the 41st
Avenue entrance. Cans of beer were being passed from hand to
hand, and raucous laughter was interspersed with loud conver-
sation, frequent swearing, and the jingle of coins. A haze of
cigaret smoke hung in the warm, heavy air. I was about to
inform Al, who was sweeping up near the handball courts, but
he'd already noticed them. He came striding over, exclaiming,
"Now I caught those palookas right in the act. Boy, would I
like to give them a piece of my mind!"

I felt a slight tightening in my stomach. A wall of eyes
confronted us as we approached the bench. "All right, you
guys, break it up right now!" Al ordered.

A husky blonde man, with a ducktail haircut and a large
orthopedic shoe on his left foot, said innocently, "Aw, c'mon,
Al. We're just sittin' here mindin' our own business and tryin'
to keep cool for Chrissakes. . . ."

"Look, I don't want a hard time from you, Butch, or
none of the rest of you," Al snapped, leveling an index finger
at him. "You know that gambling is prohibited inside the
playground so take your cards and your beer somewhere else."
He jerked his thumb toward the open gate.

A heavyset fellow with a puffy, freckled face complained,
"Hey Al, I thought you were a nice guy. The other parkies
around here let you play cards and drink beer as long as you're
not botherin' no one else."

"Yeah, Al, that's right," a few others chorused.

Al shook his head in disbelief. "Oh, sure. You guys
need a break like I need a hole in the head. Last Friday I
found a whole bunch of whiskey bottles laying inside the men's
bathroom, and this morning one of the swings was all messed
up. It took me a half an hour to fix the damn thing. So you

guys keep busting my balls, and I can bust yours, too."

"Hey, Al, that ain't fair. You ain't got no proof who did those things," a small, weasel-faced boy protested.

"Oh yeah? Who else did them? The man in the moon?"

The hoods threw back their heads, slapping their thighs as they indulged in hearty laughter. Then one of the girls, a skinny, sharp-featured blonde chomping on gum, strutted over to Al. "Hi, Al, hiya doin'?" she cooed, putting her hand on his arm. "Did anyone ever tell you, Al, that you're a real cute guy?"

There was further laughter amidst shouts of "Kiss him" and "He likes you, Frances. He's blushing."

Crimson-faced, Al shook off her arm and backed away as if he'd just been touched by a leper. "Save that baloney for someone else, Frances," he snapped. "C'mon now, I'm serious. No more monkey business. Clear out of here, all of you, or I'm calling the cops."

There were assorted rumblings of protest, most of them obscene, but in a few minutes, under Al's vigilant eye, cards and beer cans had been gathered up and the vociferous group had trickled out of the playground. There was a grim look of triumph on Al's face as he turned to me. "You see, you gotta be tough with 'em, or else they'll step all over you."

"Yeah, they're quite a bunch," I replied.

He sighed and shook his head. "That girl Frances is Butch's sister, 15 years old, and she's practically grabbing my balls! Me, a married man with grown kids and grandchildren, too! It's a shame, it really is, the way kids are brought up nowadays."

Hiding a smile, I nodded weakly, uncomfortably aware that Frances intrigued me with her tight pants, skimpy blouse, and brazen behavior. I knew it was ridiculous, but lacking a girlfriend and being shy with college girls, my natural peers, I couldn't help feeling somewhat titillated by her. Of course I'd keep these inconvenient feelings to myself, though.

Around 4:30, Al provided me with detailed instructions while guiding the flag down from the pole and folding it up, which I would be doing from now on. Tomorrow I was sched-uled to come in at 11:30 and leave at 7:30, and I was already nervously anticipating problems on Tuesday evening. So while we went about locking up the bathrooms and park house, Al gave me another little pep talk about being tough right from the start.

On Tuesday I started getting acquainted with some of the younger kids who frequented the playground. There was Lennie, an exuberant five-year old who kept asking me to play just one more game of knock hockey; and Harold, the retarded 12-year old who habitually tapped my arm as he jabbered away at me and who persisted in moving his checkers in odd, unpredictable ways. Susie, with freckles and pigtails, was seven and wanted to draw. I gave her a pencil and piece of paper, promising that I would try to obtain some crayons as soon as possible. Once, about three in the afternoon, I glimpsed several of the hoods, in their pegged pants, tee shirts with rolled up sleeves, and ducktail haircuts, sauntering about on 40th Avenue.

The playground was pretty quiet when Al left at five, so I sat inside the park house and read my book of Chekhov stories. I finished one story and was starting another when I heard a dull, crashing sound followed by laughter. A shudder went through me, then a hot, irritated feeling. Damn it! I thought. If I could only sit here reading my book, pretending I hadn't heard anything. Why can't those bastards at least wait until I've gone home?

My heart was pumping furiously as I stood up, but somehow I propelled myself out of the safety of the park house. I felt a fierce dryness in my throat and swallowed once or twice. Playing cards, smoking, and guzzling beer were Butch, Frances, Tim Duffy, the heavyset boy, and Tony Carbo, an olive-skinned fellow with black, carefully pomaded hair. A trash can had been overturned, spilling a large variety of garbage across the park entrance. Anger churned inside me, and despite a pair of rather shaky knees, I marched toward the bench in my olive-green uniform. I felt their smirking eyes on me, especially the hard, bright ones of Frances, which I studiously avoided. Butch gave me a broad smile and called out in a friendly voice, "Hey, parkie, how you doin'? You want some beer?" He extended his beer can toward me as the others tittered.

Clearing my throat, in as tough a voice as I could muster, I said, "I want you to pick up all that stuff there off the ground."

There were some mock gasps of astonishment, and then Butch said, "You gotta be kiddin'. Why should we pick all that shit up?"

"Because you spilled it."

"We did not, parkie," Frances protested, red, tapered fingernails snaking through strawberry blonde hair, outlining small, firm breasts. For a moment I stared into her China blue eyes hooded with mascara and eye shadow.

Then I said to Butch, "Look, I don't want to give you guys a hard time, but I'm just trying to do my job. . . ."

"He's just trying to do his job," Butch mimicked, pitching his voice an octave or so above mine. "So let's give the new parkie a real big hand because he's just tryin' to do his job."

I felt my body go hot as they began a boisterous round of applause and whistling. Angrily I shouted, "Look, if you don't leave right now, I'm calling the cops."

The noise died down, and Butch looked hard at me for a moment with opaque, bloodshot blue eyes. Then the big grin came over his craggy face, and he said in his mocking voice, "Gee whiz, whattaya know, parkie's gonna call the cops. That ain't a very friendly thing to do now, is it, parkie?"

Howling with laughter, the hoods spilled beer and knocked cards to the ground. I felt a taut sensation gathering in my chest. I strode out of the playground toward the call box on Bowne and 41st. But when I reached the corner and confronted the small white box, I suddenly felt the anger drain out of me. I don't want to become a police informer unless the situation gets a lot more serious than this, I decided. I waited a few minutes, then walked nervously back to the playground. To my great relief, the hoods had vanished, probably through the gate on the Sanford Avenue side of the playground. Rather pleased with myself, I got Al's broom and dustpan and swept up the debris scattered over the ground.

I played a few games of knock hockey with Lenny and

his nine-year old sister, Sandra, then around seven began my efforts at hauling down the flag. By now I'd entirely forgotten Al's careful instructions, and the flag refused to budge despite my swearing and pleading with it. For a few desperate moments I even considered leaving it up, though I knew Al would be quite displeased with this breach of established procedure. Finally, however, after a combination of some strenuous and lucky maneuvering, I was relieved to see the flag slide cleanly down the pole and into my cramped hands. When I left the playground that evening, the weary ache in my arms and legs told me that I'd genuinely earned my pay.

On Wednesday, I recounted to Al my triumphant first encounter with the hoods. "Next time call the cops if those wise bastards keep bustin' your balls," he advised me. "Once they think you're soft, they'll really make life miserable for you." He did add, however, that I was doing a much better job than my predecessor, Bernie Finkelstein, who'd just let the hoods do whatever they'd pleased, devoting several hours of each day to cooking elaborate meals in the park house.

"I suppose he got fired," I said.

"Honest to Pete, he really should have been, Steve!" Al declared. "But no, he resigned. He was a big, fat guy, probably over 250 pounds, you know, and Frances and some of the other kids teased the poor guy to death. They made his life so miserable that after a while he just gave up. He never should have been working here in the first place."

That afternoon some of the hoods were playing handball, even Butch, who seemed to play fairly well, though his limp obviously hampered him. Sometimes after he'd missed a shot, the sounds of Butch's furious swearing echoed through the whole playground, as if he were shaking everything to its very foundation. The hoods weren't drinking, however, so Al and I merely kept a wary eye on them. When they left the playground shortly after four, both of us visibly relaxed.

Soon after Al's departure at five, the recreation supervisor, Ted Birnbaum, paid me a visit. He was a short, round, cherubic-looking man with tortoise shell glasses. We introduced ourselves, and he gave me a warm smile and handshake.

Then we sat down at the table in the park house, and he asked me how things were going. I hesitated, then said, "O.K., I guess. I like a lot of the kids here. . . . I haven't organized any tournaments yet, though. . . . There's a bunch of tough kids, you know, that are kind of hard to work with. . . ."

Birnbaum nodded. "That's true, this is a tough playground to work in, Steve. Just do the best you can. If you like kids, that's the main thing." He paused exploring thinning, light-brown hair with pudgy fingers, then resumed. "You know, I've been working for the Park Department for twelve years now, and frankly, I don't expect miracles any more. I guess I'm just older and wearier now." He sighed softly and patted his flushed, perspiring face with a handkerchief.

Then Birnbaum picked up my book of Chekhov stories. "So you're reading Chekhov?" he asked, giving me a conspiratorial sort of smile.

"Yes, he's one of my favorite writers."

"I read some of his stories and plays a long time ago," the supervisor said, leafing through the book, then laying it down and sighing. "I feel guilty not having reread him all these years. I know I should do more reading, but when I come home from work, I'm tired so instead of reading a book, I turn on the television set. It's a wonder my brain hasn't turned completely to putty by now." He shook his head despondently.

Concealing a smile, I murmured sympathetic words. Birnbaum was a rather strange supervisor; with his gentle, resigned sadness he reminded me of a Chekhov character himself.

The supervisor asked me where I was going to school and what I was studying. When I told him, he eagerly confessed his own desire to return to school someday. Then he offered me some gum drops, which I politely declined, watching as he crammed the bright, powdery candies into his mouth. "Candy and crappy food, that's my downfall," he declared forlornly. "I should lose at least 20 pounds, and this isn't helping. I guess it comes from being a bachelor and falling into bad eating habits. What I need is a good woman."

We talked for a while about one thing and another, women, Chekhov, Erich Fromm, movies and television programs, hardly mentioning anything at all about the job. Then Birnbaum glanced at the clock and moaned, "My God, it's 6:30 already. I still have two more playgrounds to visit. I've enjoyed our conversation very much, Steve. Maybe tonight I'll read a book instead of turning on the television set."

As I watched him plod off like a gentle, roundshouldered bear, I felt lucky that I was here just for the summer instead of a lifetime. In any event, I could relax about organizing things since Birnbaum obviously didn't care about that. When I ventured outside, I was relieved to discover no sign of the hoods. I felt as if I'd been given a reprieve that evening when I left the playground without having had to assert my authority even once.

Over the next few weeks, I came to realize that the hoods were leaving me alone, though every once in a while I felt compelled to reprimand them for some infraction or other. The job had already settled into a routine of sorts, slightly tense at times but manageable. During the early afternoons, I supervised and played with the younger kids and talked to Al, listening to his complaints about the playground, or about the growing state of moral decay in our society. Occasionally, as a change of pace, he related wry anecdotes about the playground and about Park Department politics. Once he proudly displayed for me pictures from his wallet of his children and grandchildren, eagerly answering my polite questions about them. After five, I usually tried to relax with a book inside the park house, surfacing every so often to make sure everything was in order. About every week or so, I had leisurely chats with Birnbaum.

One balmy afternoon, feeling somewhat bored, I hung around by the handball courts, watching Butch and Tony play doubles against Bill and Mike, two peripheral members of the group. None of the players seemed to pay much attention to me; but when the game was over, Bill, one of the winners, said, "Hey, parkie, you want the next game?"

I hesitated, not sure whether he was being serious, then heard myself saying yes. I picked Tony as my partner since he was a better player than Butch.

At first I played nervously and erratically, and we fell far behind. "You better hang up your jockstrap right now, parkie, and go sit in the park house with Al," Butch called out from the sidelines, and the other players guffawed, including my partner, Tony.

Stung by their derision, I vowed to show them I could play. Concentrating intently, I began controlling my shots and even hitting some killers. When we'd tied the score at 15-15 after I'd put the ball just beyond Bill's reach, Butch exclaimed, "Goddamn, the parkie does know how to play! You can forget what I said about hangin' up your jockstrap." Exhilarated by Butch's compliment, I smiled briefly, then prepared to hit my next serve. Soon Tony and I had won a hard-fought game, 21-18.

"Nice goin', parkie. You played like a champ," Tony exulted, clapping me on the back.

"Good game," Bill said, as he and Mike shook hands with us.

I sensed that all of them viewed me with new respect now. I played two more games of doubles that afternoon, both hotly contested, winning the first and losing the second. I enjoyed the vigorous exercise, the first real athletic workout I'd had at the playground. But more important, I could now relax with the hoods a little bit. I made tentative attempts to participate in their banter, delighted when my hesitant sallies were rewarded with generous laughter. When I left the playground that evening, I hummed, and my step was unaccustomedly light.

From then on, I played handball frequently with Butch and his crowd, though I was also careful to attend to my various duties, as well as invariably to conform to the playground rules myself. Even after Al had gone home, I always declined any beer that was offered me and never played handball for money despite occasional attempts to coax me to do so. Sometimes I felt myself wavering in these situations but decided that as long as I went by the rules, there was nothing Al could legitimately do to me. I was beginning to view Butch and his crowd as distinct individuals rather than "the hoods." Several times I caught Al regarding me with a puzzled frown, though he didn't say anything directly to me concerning my new associations. I was secretly gratified by his silent discomfort; yet at times I had the uneasy feeling that I was walking a tightrope, precariously poised between my awkward relationship with Al and my somewhat nebulous one with Butch and his pals.

Sometimes Frances hung around during the handball games, languidly combing her long, heavy hair, freshening lipstick or face powder, giggling with her girlfriends, and exchanging repartee, as well as playful kicks and pokes with the boys. Her presence was disturbingly arousing, causing me occasional lapses of concentration during the game, and at other times making me play somewhat harder than usual in order to impress her. Still, I was polite but distant whenever she smiled or spoke to me, recalling Al's insistent words that first day about behaving cautiously with the girls in the playground.

One slow, steamy afternoon in early August when Al, having had some personal business to attend to, had gone out during his lunch hour, I sat in the park house reading. After a while, there was a knock on the door. I got up and opened it. Frances and her friend, Debbie, a plump brunette, were standing there, smacking gum and beaming brightly at me.

"Hi, parkie. Hiya doin'?" Frances said in her high, shrill voice.

"Hi," I replied coolly.

"Can we come in and look at the equipment? We want something to play with," she informed me, one hand arched casually on her hip, big blue eyes flashing boldly into mine. She was wearing blue cutoffs, a sleeveless yellow cotton blouse, and loafers.

I pushed away the faint stirring of sexual excitement within me. Damn it! I thought. Why couldn't Frances look ugly? Why does she have to have such shapely arms and legs, such a nice body to torment me? "What do you want? I can tell you if we have it," I said in my official voice.

Frances shrugged. "We don't know what we want, parkie, so that's why we wanna look around. . . ."

"I'm sorry, but you're not supposed to."

Her voice was low and intimate as she poked knuckles into my ribs. "Aw, c'mon, parkie, don't be a louse. Just for a couple of minutes. O.K? Al won't find out."

"How do you know he won't?"

" 'Cause Al just went to lunch, that's why. He won't be back till one o'clock, I betcha. . . . Hey, you want some gum, parkie?" She offered me a crumpled stick of Juicy Fruit she'd just dug out of her pocket.

I shook my head. "No thanks."

Frances looked hurt, as if I'd just rejected her expensive Christmas present. "Well, parkie, whattaya say?" she demanded. "We don't got all day, y'know. Just for a couple of minutes. O.K? I promise." She pressed her hand over her heart, nudging her resilient breast.

A twinge of desire assailed my groin. I began smiling as I thought of putting one over on Al, breaking his strongest injunction, leeting a girl inside the park house. I was sick and tired of following every one of his petty rules, as if I were a grade school child. "All right," I conceded. "But just for a few minutes. O.K?"

"Sure, we promise," Frances said quickly as the girls clattered inside.

"And don't tell anyone I let you in," I added, shutting the door, then glancing at the clock. It was almost 25 minutes after twelve. The chances were that Al wouldn't be back for at least 20 minutes. I felt the exhilaration of a gambler betting everything on one decisive spin of the wheel. My pulses raced as I contemplated my own daring.

I stood off to the side, watching the girls examine the recreational equipment, laughing and making disparaging comments about everything they inspected. I bit my lip to control the erection gripping me as I stared at the two juicy globes tautly molded by Frances' cutoffs. Jesus! I thought. I really want to kiss her now, and I think she wants me to also. But Debbie's here, damn it! Besides, if Al finds out, I'll get fired. No, I better tell them to leave right now. But the minutes went by, and I gazed helplessly at Frances, unable to summon up the will to ask her to go. When I glanced anxiously at the clock, I noted with alarm that it was 20 minutes to one. I stammered that it was time for the girls to depart, but Frances gave me a mocking smile, which caused me to turn red, as I figured she was taunting me for my lack of nerve, my tongue-tied timidity.

"Hey, parkie, you got a jump rope?" she demanded.

"No, but I can try to get one."

"But I want one now," Frances insisted, stamping her foot and continuing to stare challengingly into my eyes.

"Look, I'm sorry . . . I'll try to. . . ." I fumbled, feeling like a mental retard.

"Hey, you got some tennis rackets, then?" Her tongue slithered over her upper lip, as she patted into place stray wisps of strawberry blonde hair.

"No, we don't have those either. But next time the recreation supervisor comes, I'll. . . ."

"What kind of crummy playground is this, anyway? You don't have anything," Frances complained as Debbie giggled.

I'll have to do something right now, I thought desperately. Either insist that she leave or kiss her. Kiss her? I must be out of my mind. She might slap me, or worse, laugh in my face. Besides, I'll probably lose my job. Once again, I mumbled something about the girls' having to leave, sighing heavily when they paid no more heed to my hesitant command than the previous time. Taking a deep breath and trying to ignore the stubborn hammering of my heart and the hot coating of sweat that seemed to have erupted over most of my body, I moved toward Frances. Her eyes, large and glittering, watched me with a non-commital smile. My tentative kiss was answered by her strong, firm one as she clasped her arms around my neck. Debbie was tittering, but neither of us paid much attention. Responding to the teasing pressure of her tongue and lips, I explored the hospitable cavern of Frances' mouth with my own tongue. As I was giddily running my hand through her thick hair, I froze as I heard the click of a key in the lock. Frances broke free from my grasp. The door swung open, and Al was staring at us, a horrified expression on his face. I wanted to shrivel up and vanish right then.

"Hey, what the hell's going on here?" he demanded, wide eyes swiftly taking in Frances' disheveled appearance, then darting back to me. The lipstick smears on my face and the bulge in my pants must have told him the whole story.

I tried to speak, but the words wouldn't come. Carefully rearranging her hair, Frances said casually, "The parkie just let us in so we could see what we wanted, Al. That's all."

Al glowered at her. "Oh yeah? Well for your information, no one who isn't a park employee is allowed in here. So go on, scram, both of you!"

"But, Al," she began.

"Get the hell out!" he roared, his hand making a sweeping gesture toward the door.

Muttering under her breath, Frances stalked out, followed by Debbie. Al slammed the door, and I heard the muffled sound of laughter outside. He gestured brusquely toward a chair. "Sit down!"

I felt my whole body shaking and drenched with sweat as I collapsed onto the chair. Al tossed his black lunchbox and his *Daily News* onto the table, then sat down hard opposite me. His eyes blazed as he brought his fist down on the table. "For crying out loud, Steve, didn't I tell you about this stuff the first day you were here?"

I nodded morosely, eyes lowered. "Yes," I murmured.

"So what the hell did you let them in here for?"

I felt his narrowed, merciless eyes probing me. Shifting about in my chair, I sensed the futility of my whole situation. I looked directly at Al and said, "All right, I know it was dumb. I'll resign."

"Tell me the truth," he said. "I don't want any bullshit. What were you and Frances doing inside the park house?"

I sighed. He probably knew, anyway. "I kissed her," I confessed.

Al's face tightened. "You're damn straight you're resigning," he shouted. "And how long has this monkey business been going on, playing around with that little tramp? I'll bet this isn't the first time."

I felt anger surging up within me. "This is the first time," I insisted, trying to keep my voice level. "So don't go getting your dirty mind all in an uproar."

Flushing beet red, Al glared incredulously at me, clench-his fists. "What? What the fuck did you just say, you smart-ass son-of-a-bitch?"

"You heard what I said," I retorted, astounded by my own audacity, nervously wondering whether Al was going to jump up and hit me.

He scowled at me some more, as if trying to decide what to do; then, mumbling fiercely, he jerked up and strode toward the phone. As I listened to Al denounce me to one of the Park Department higher-ups, I considered appealing to Birnbaum, soon deciding, however, it would be futile. Birnbaum was part of the system, too. I don't care about this stupid job any more, and I'm definitely not going to apologize for kissing Frances, I vowed. Al deserved what I gave him; it was long overdue. Now I'll just have to think of something to tell my parents.

The rest of the afternoon consisted mainly of a tedious, unreal series of dealings with Al and the Park Department bureaucracy. With unaccustomed haste, they hustled me out of their employment as if they'd just discovered I was on the Ten Most Wanted list. At The Arsenal, the main office in Central Park, I signed papers stating that my resignation was effective starting tomorrow. Fortunately, I didn't encounter Birnbaum, as both of us would have been quite embarrassed, I felt.

Though tired and drained, I returned to the playground after five to say goodbye to Butch, Frances, and the others. "Hey, you were the best fuckin' parkie we had in a long time," Butch declared, pounding me on the back. "Hell, you shouldn't of let 'em make you quit for Chrissakes! You should of told 'em to fire that dumb fuckhead, Al, instead. The lousy cock-

sucker! We would of all stood behind you on that." Butch's
friends cheered in agreement.

Moved by their support, I said, "Thanks, I really appreci-
ate that. But I don't think it would have done much good.
Al has a lot more pull in the Park Department than I have,
you know."

I drank a couple of beers with them, taking some good-
natured kidding about Frances; then, after a little bit of coax-
ing, I kissed her, to the accompaniment of prolonged applause.
But I felt self-conscious with her now, as if someone else had
been kissing Frances in the park house. A wave of sadness
swept over me as I reflected that her bony face was still a
child's, however hard amateurishly applied makeup worked to
deny it. Despite her toughness, she had an appealing quality
of innocence that would probably be gone in only a few years.
The full impact of being fired from the job had finally hit me.
All I wanted to do was go home and sleep. I felt that I, like
Frances, was a child trying to cope with a difficult, sometimes
overwhelming adult world.

NO, I MEAN HE'S A NEGRO

I WAS UPSTAIRS IN MY ROOM that evening, devouring Stendhal's *The Red and the Black*, intoxicated by Julien Sorel's audacious love affair with an older married woman, Madame de Renal. For a few delirious hours I would inhabit Julien's magical realm, banishing the fact that I was merely a timid, confused 21-year old schoolboy living at home with his parents. I had just graduated from Queens College and in the fall was scheduled to begin graduate studies in English at Columbia. I was sick of school and sterile, pedantic English departments, desiring instead to start living authentically and become a writer. But my parents had persuaded me that I'd be a fool to throw away a scholarship and surrender myself to the army for two bleak years. It was 1961, and staying in school until you were 26 seemed about the most foolproof way to beat the draft. Mortgaging five more years of my life to academic tedium appeared an acceptable price to pay to avoid the violence and mindlessness of the army. Intending to take it easy the whole summer, I figured by the fall I'd be reconciled to the prospect of resuming the academic grind.

I was in the midst of an absorbing passage about Julien and Madame de Renal when my mother called me downstairs, informing me that I had visitors. I read several more sentences, then with a sigh put down my book. In the living room, I shook hands warmly with Peter Friedman and Sam Cohen. I hadn't seen either of them in quite a while and was a bit surprised, as well as amused, by the black felt hat sporting a red feather which was set at a rakish angle on Peter's dark, curly head. But then, Peter seemed to be trying hard to break out of his shell. For the past few months, he'd been hanging around with a bunch of zany bohemian types and had also taken a leave of absence from Queens College.

My mother served us pretzels and ginger ale in the living room. When she asked my friends what they were doing now, Peter looked blank and merely shrugged, but Sam said eagerly, "I'll be doing some tutoring during the summer, Mrs. Maltz. And in the fall I'll be going to Cornell to work toward a doctorate in history.

My mother nodded and smiled. "That's great, Sam! Cornell has an excellent reputation. Steve's going to Columbia in the fall with a Regents College Teaching Fellowship. I don't think he quite appreciates yet how lucky he is to be getting a scholarship and going to such a fine school and not having to worry about the army snapping him up."

I sighed. "Look, do you want me to kiss the ground?"

"No, just buckle down to work in the fall and get your Ph. D., that's what I want you to do," my mother shot back.

"That's all? How about a little post-doctoral degree thrown in after that?" I demanded.

My mother threw up her hands. "All right, let's just drop the whole subject. I'm going back to watching that Galsworthy play on television. Make yourselves comfortable here. There's more ginger ale in the refrigerator."

"Yeah, thanks," I said quickly, relieved when she'd left.

Sam, who was short and sandy-haired with a pale, freckled complexion, reached for the bowl of pretzels on the coffee table. For a while there was just the sound of pretzels being crunched. Then I said, "I guess I'm just a little bit tired of school right now, that's all. Sometimes I feel as if I've been going to school non-stop ever since I've been born. Besides, the only thing you can do with English is teach, and I don't really think I'm cut out for teaching, anyway. . . . I guess it's the same thing with history, isn't it?"

Sam nodded. "Yeah. But I wouldn't mind teaching on a college level. You don't have to worry there all the time about discipline and motivation. And I enjoy history, so actually, I'd be getting paid for something I like to do anyway, shooting my mouth off about it."

I smiled but couldn't help feeling some dislike for Sam, tinged with envy. I restrained myself from saying something nasty about academia, from attempting to puncture Sam's apparent self-assurance about his future. Instead I said, "Yeah, I guess it isn't too bad once you get through graduate school."

"Grad school is supposed to be a lot more interesting and challenging, on a considerably higher level than college," Sam declared. "You have a lot more say over what you study; they treat you more like an adult. Besides, in my book, grad school sure as hell beats the army."

"Yeah, in mine, too," I said, aware that my voice lacked complete conviction.

There was a pause, and I glanced at Peter, who seemed light years away already, his soft, sad eyes abstracted behind hornrimmed glasses. Obviously, he wasn't enjoying this conversation about graduate school since he was having enough trouble right now just finishing college.

"So what have you been up to?" I asked him.

"Ah, not much," he mumbled, shrugging. His narrow, olive-skinned face was impassive, expressing the futility of trying to communicate his own private vision to the outside world.

There was another pause, and I decided to bring the conversation around to politics. Despite everything, Peter clung fiercely to his politics like a wino to his last drink. I wasn't disappointed. Soon a full-scale political conversation was underway, with Peter right in the middle of it.

"Castro's essentially a dictator, even though he pretends he's a man of the people. You know, he makes five hour speeches. The guy's a narcissist; he must really be in love with the sound of his own voice," Sam was saying.

"If Castro were just another dictator, he would have gone along with the United States government and the corporations," I retorted.

"Yeah, yeah, that's right," Peter added, head bobbing, his face animated now. His words erupted in a staccato burst. "And, you know, how come if Castro's a dictator, then how come he goes around the country and talks to the common people all the time, you know? . . . It's to educate the people, that's why. . . . Like if he didn't care, you know, he wouldn't bother talking for five hours. . . ."

Sam laughed. "Educate the people? You mean brainwash them. He's already turned the country into a Russian satellite.

Peter waved disgustedly. "Ah, get out of there! That's just capitalist propaganda. The Russians are, like they're for all the working people everywhere, you know, so that's why they're helping Cuba against the American government."

The argument continued, mainly between Peter and Sam. I didn't seem to feel as strongly about the subject as either of them. I recalled that memorable first encounter several years ago at the Queens College N.A.A.C.P. chapter, where Peter had made groping, painful attempts to say what everyone else was saying. Yet despite that, I had been drawn to him, perhaps partly because Peter's awkward intensity had reminded me of my own. Besides, Peter's sweetness and gentleness weren't common qualities among the left wing crowd. Shy and unsure of ourselves in the aggressive world of politics, Peter and I were destined to remain on the fringes of campus left wing circles. Still, it had been fun hanging around together on N.A.A.C.P. picket lines, at peace marches, Fair Play for Cuba rallies, and folk song hootenannies. We had both come from politically active families. Though sometimes bored and frustrated by Peter's frequent difficulties in communicating, I felt

closer to him than to Sam, who would probably someday be-
come a rather dull, mildly liberal, and fairly competent college
teacher.

After a while, feeling myself tiring of the discussion, I
suggested taking a walk. Sam and Peter, who seemed to sense
a political stalemate, readily accepted my suggestion. I went
to inform my parents in the television room. "Please be sensible and
don't stay out too late, Steve. You know what the bums are
like in this neighborhood," my mother told me.

"Yeah, sure," I said impatiently. My mother was always
making something out of nothing.

Going up Parsons Boulevard, the three of us turned left
on 59th Avenue. The early June air was warm and placid. At
nine on a weekday night, this semi-suburban neighborhood
was usually pretty quiet. Tonight there was only the occasion-
al howl of a dog or the dialogue from a television serial carry-
ing into the street. I was struck by Peter's appearance as we
ambled along 59th Avenue, turning right on 159th Street. His
hat, cocked slightly over his right eye, along with neatly pres-
sed blue gabardine slacks, and a shiny black zippered jacket,
made Peter look uncharacteristically flamboyant, a little like
a gambler. In contrast, I was wearing tan chino pants and a
plain cotton jacket, and Sam wore faded corduroys and an old
sweatshirt. I thought about Peter's new friends, some of whom
I knew slightly, and I was curious about how they accepted
Peter, as well as a little envious of the new adventures he must
be having.

"So do you see those guys much, you know, Lenny and
Kevin and that crowd?" I asked him.

Peter's face lit up. "Just once in a while, I guess. They're
a great bunch of guys. They know how to, you know, like
have a good time. Sometimes they have real wild parties, you
know, like orgies, I guess."

Sam and I exchanged startled glances. It wasn't easy vis-
ualizing Peter taking part in an orgy. "What happens at one
of those orgies?" Sam asked.

"Well, like last week, you know, they had a couple of
girls over at Kevin's place, and they had all this wine and beer

and some marijuana, you know, that stuff you smoke. . . .
Kevin was playing the guitar, and everyone was singing and
dancing, and like some people took their clothes off and did
things in front of everyone. . . . And this one guy John, you
know, he threw up all over the place. He must have drunk, I
don't know, nearly a gallon of wine or something. . . . He
likes to do stuff like pull down his pants in front of nuns."

Sam and I burst out laughing. But then Sam's face turn-
ed serious. "I think he's disgusting. He sounds pretty juvenille
to me."

"He's a lot of fun. He just does, you know, whatever he
feels like," Peter retorted.

"Did you take part in everything?" I asked, repelled yet
also intrigued by the scene Peter had described.

"Nah," Peter said. "Like I had a glass of wine or two and
a little marijuana, you know, but mostly I just watched. The
other guys, like they don't mind or anything."

I nodded, pity replacing my envy. Peter's friends prob-
ably found him merely an amusing curiosity.

On 159th Street, we turned the corner onto a block along-
side the Horace Harding Expressway, consisting mostly of
closed stores. At the end of the short block, three young,
tough-looking white men stood outside a bar and watched a
black man escorting a white woman to a taxi parked down the
block. She was heavily made-up and wore a blonde wig and
low-cut dress, looking like a prostitute. The black man, stocky
and well-dressed, seemed around 40. Laughing, buoyant with
drink, they'd apparently just left the bar. An interracial couple
in this neighborhood was an unusual event, and the three
toughs stood with clenched fists and taut faces, exchanging a
few barbed words with the black man. I felt my pulses race
with curiosity and overtones of menace. I thought suddenly
of Julien Sorel defiantly carrying on an affair with Madame de
Renal right under her self-important husband's nose.

"Hey, mac, is the cab driver a nigger, too?" someone
called out in a rough, drunken voice. My body tightened, and
I looked straight ahead, pretending I hadn't heard.

The black, seated beside the woman now, slammed the

back door; the taxi started up and pulled away from the curb. The voice came again, louder, with a tinge of impatience now. "Hey, mac, I said is the cab driver a nigger, too?"

Peter, Sam, and I glanced over at the husky blonde man who was unmistakably addressing us. He had a ducktail hair-cut and wore blue jeans and a tee shirt with rolled-up sleeves. His companions had just re-entered the bar. The ensuing silence was an infinity, the blonde man's question hanging heavily in the air, demanding acquiescence in his view of the world.

"Yes, the cab driver's a Negro," Peter suddenly replied, startling me.

"You mean he's a nigger, don't you?" the tough smilingly corrected.

"No, I mean he's a Negro," Peter persisted, emphatically shaking his head, smiling in turn. He and the other man exchanged grinning stares for several moments as the three of us went past the bar. The whole thing felt unreal, like a dream. Was this the same Peter who usually just shrugged and looked blank? Sam whispered to Peter not to say anything more, but Peter didn't seem to hear.

The blonde man, an incongruous grin frozen to his hard, flushed face, leveled an index finger at Peter. "He's a nigger, mac, and you're gonna learn that if you don't know that by now." His words still sounded like banter, however, despite the slight edge to them now.

"No, you'll learn," Peter retorted, pointing his finger, too, and continuing to smile, as if this were merely some amusing, childish game.

The man mumbled something and disappeared into the bar. A feeling of relief passed through me. Still, Peter had seemed rather foolhardy.

"You know, you shouldn't have answered him back," Sam said.

"Yeah, but that guy, like he called Negroes niggers, you know, so I had to say something. They're people, you know, just like everyone else."

"Of course. I know that," Sam said. "But he didn't exactly seem as if he was interested in being educated.

Actually, I'm surprised he didn't want to fight."

I was about to agree with Sam, yet also praise Peter for his nerve, when a raw, drunken cry interrupted me. "Fuckin' bastard!" Shaking his fist, the blonde man accompanied by three companions, strode across the street in our direction.

We continued walking at the same pace, though I felt myself beginning to tremble. The toughs would probably just try to scare us a little. The thing to do now was agree with everything they said, even apologize if necessary.

"Hey, you niggerloving bastard! I'm gonna kill you!" the man called from perhaps twenty yards away. My heart fluttered violently, and my knees shook. Damn it! I thought. We should have run as soon as the guy had gone back into the bar. But now it's too late. I stopped and turned, trying to appear unruffled. Peter and Sam also turned to face our pursuers. The bull-necked blonde man, breathing thickly, stepped from the cluster of his companions and stabbed a finger at Peter. "That's him, the fuckin' niggerlover!"

I clenched my fists, reluctantly prepared to defend myself, but the man's friends stayed put. The tough lurched forward, grunting as he swung at Peter. I winced as knuckles crunched against bone and flesh, staggering Peter, jarring the hat from his head. The hoods laughed harshly, producing an abrupt, joyless noise. How vulnerable Peter looked, a gaunt, bespectacled sleepwalker at the mercy of his burly assailant! There was a cold, queasy knot in my stomach. I cursed my own softness, my terror of fighting, the sheltered existence I led, living at home with my parents, always reading books, eternally going to school.

The next blow sent Peter's glasses flying, clinking to the sidewalk. Peter blinked helplessly, and another mirthless laugh greeted his naked, bewildered face. Clenching my fists, I tried to whip myself into a churning rage; but one quick glance at the hard, stolid faces of the three onlookers standing shoulder to shoulder, cigarets dangling from the tight lips of two of them, brought the nauseous feeling back into my stomach. One of them was a short man, almost a midget, and for a moment I found myself hypnotized by his hard eyes, taut

mouth, and beaked nose. Then I sighed and pulled my eyes
away. No, shorty, too, would probably be pretty tough in a
fight, I decided. The shuttered houses, the quietness of the
street despite the adjacent expressway, made it seem futile
to yell for help.

A flurry of blows missed their mark; the tough, grunting
loudly, seemed a bit tired already. I started to relax, but then
a punch thudded against Peter's jaw, tatooing a tiny patch of
pink into his soft brown skin. "Hey!" Peter exclaimed, back-
ing away, finally appearing to realize that the hood actually
wanted to hurt him.

"Cocksucker!" his attacker gloated.

Peter hunched beneath upraised arms, like a tortoise
underneath its shell, though he still didn't attempt to fight
back. Sam and I exchanged relieved glances. He beckoned
me aside, then whispered, "We better call the cops."

"Maybe we should try to help him first," I suggested.

Sam stared at me. "Are you crazy? Those guys are all
street fighters."

I looked once more at the three companions, then
nodded and said, "Yeah, all right."

Sam and I ran hard, panting as we pulled up at another
bar, two blocks away at 163rd Street. Inside, Sam used the
pay phone. Pacing back and forth, I listened as he seemed to
be having to convince the police that the situation was urgent.
Finally Sam hung up.

"The bastards! They won't come, I bet," I said.

"They said they would. Besides, what else could we do?"
Sam demanded. "Those guys probably carry knives."

"Yeah, I wouldn't be surprised. Anyway, I hope Peter's
still in one piece."

"They knew we were calling the police, so maybe they've
quit by now," Sam said.

Cautiously we returned. The block was eerily deserted.
I picked up Peter's glasses. One of the frames was broken, and
the right lens was cracked. Sam retrieved Peter's hat, slightly
battered, and minus its red feather.

"Jesus, where the hell is he?" I demanded.

"He's probably right around here. We were only gone a few minutes," Sam said.

We went hurriedly past the bar, aware of a wall of stony faces staring out at us. Then we turned the corner on 159th Street. A little bit ahead, Peter was stumbling in the direction of my house. We ran up to him.

"Are you O.K?" I asked, relieved, yet still worried.

"Are you all right, Peter?" Sam repeated, louder, when he didn't answer immediately.

Peter's voice was almost a whisper. "Yeah . . . I don't know . . . maybe . . . it hurts a little, I guess." Gingerly he fingered his pale face, flecked with pink patches but surprisingly unbloodied. The bruised skin, the soft, dazed eyes made me want to laugh and cry at the same time. The ironic thought came to me that Peter probably didn't have any black friends at all.

"Where does it hurt? Can you walk all right?" Sam asked.

"My chest hurts a little, but I can walk O.K., I guess," Peter said, wincing. His lips were purple, and his teeth were chattering.

I handed him the damaged glasses, and Sam gave him his hat. Wearing his glasses, Peter looked slightly less bewildered. The hat, rumpled and askew on his tousled head, didn't look jaunty now.

"What happened? How did you get away?" I asked.

"The other guys, they, they pulled him off me after he knocked me down. They, they said it was enough, you know, like he might really hurt me."

"That was lucky!" I exclaimed, surprised that those hard exteriors concealed human feelings. Or maybe they'd merely been afraid the police would come.

"We called the cops. Let's go back and see if they came," Sam said.

Peter shook his head. "Nah, it's O.K. Like it's over with now, you know."

"But that guy was really trying to hurt you, Peter. He could have killed you!" Sam insisted.

"Yeah, I know. But it's over with now," Peter repeated

impassively.

"All right, then," Sam conceded. "But I still think he shouldn't be allowed to get away with it."

Peter didn't say anything. I recalled stories I'd heard of Peter's recent turn toward religion, donning prayer shawl and phylacteries in the early morning darkness and praying for hours. He'd probably pray for his assailant now.

We walked back to my house, where we proceeded to give a breathless account of the incident to my parents. I felt my mother's eyes resting disappointedly on me, as if I'd been responsible for things by not having heeded her earlier warning.

My father's face was taut and pale. "I have a good mind to go back there right now. Those lousy bastards deserve to have their goddamn heads bashed in!" he shouted.

Wishing I had my father's courage, I shuddered, picturing my father, Sam, and me being surrounded, then submerged by a horde of hoods.

"Howard, please, don't go back there!" my mother implored. "It's insane starting in with those bums all over again. It's more important to get Peter to the hospital right away."

My father sighed. "Yeah, I guess you're right. Still, I hate to see those bastards get off scot-free."

My mother gave Peter a blanket to wrap around him. Then my father drove Peter to the emergency ward of Booth Memorial Hospital. There, Sam, my father, and I waited grimly on a bench while Peter was being examined. A heavy silence prevailed among us. I hope he doesn't have any internal injuries, I thought, getting up and beginning to pace back and forth, making frequent trips to the water fountain. I felt oppressed by the hospital's atmosphere of sterile remoteness, by the harassed voice and face of the nurse attending to Peter. I told myself again and again that Peter deserved what he'd gotten, that he'd been a fool to argue with a tough and then be totally unprepared for the hood's logical rejoinder. Still, I could not rid myself of a pervasive sense of guilt, the feeling that Sam and I had somehow failed Peter. Were we the cowardly opportunists and Peter the man of principle? I kept asking myself.

Finally, a little after midnight, the nurse informed us, "There don't seem to be any internal injuries as far as we can tell right now, but there are definitely some broken bones. Several ribs are fractured, and his nose is broken. Also there looks as if there might be a break in the left clavicle. We'll have to keep him in the hospital at least overnight. . . ."

I didn't hear the rest of what she said or my father's replies to her. There was a dull, throbbing ache in my head, and I wanted to sleep for days. Though greatly relieved that Peter's injuries weren't critical, nevertheless, I was stunned by the extent of them.

Sam and I visited Peter frequently in the next few weeks. He seemed to be recuperating rather well from his various fractures, the most serious of which was the broken collarbone. And despite his parents' disapproval, he still went out to visit his bohemian friends. But our visits were otherwise disappointing. While his mother called him "sweetie" and "dearie" and plied him with food and drink, his father kept badgering Peter to acknowledge his mistakes in the incident and agree to have his attacker sought and arrested. And Peter, in turn, repeatedly shook his head, flatly stating that he considered the whole affair closed. When alone with Sam and me, Peter was pleasant enough but said nothing, looking blank whenever Sam or I referred to the traumatic event. I didn't feel that anything had been resolved, however. I continued to play and replay the entire sequences of events over in my mind, searching for reasons and answers.

One overcast afternoon when Sam and I had just left Peter's house in Forest Hills and were walking toward the bus stop, I said, "I wonder why we keep visiting Peter; he's turned into a real zombie."

"I don't think he's able to look at why he acted the way he did, so he just refuses to talk about it," Sam replied. "He's obviously depressed."

"Yeah, he seems to be," I agreed. "O.K., so why do you think he acted the way he did?"

A faint smile appeared on Sam's austere face. "Well, I think Peter has the strong guilt feelings towards Negroes that a lot of whites have, especially political types. It's as if Peter felt he had to take complete responsibility for the whole racial situation right then, as if he were offering himself as some sort of sacrifice. . . . It's absurd, though. Is Peter totally responsible for the unsatisfactory situation of Negroes in this country just because his skin happens to be white?"

"But certainly whites have some responsibility to try to change things," I protested. "After all, we as whites have certain privileges in American society because people with darker skin in this country and other countries are being oppressed by white people."

"That's true up to a certain point," Sam retorted. "But I still think you need to draw the line somewhere between reasonable individual responsibility and indiscriminate guilt."

We continued arguing, even as we boarded the bus. I considered that Sam was mainly trying to justify his own inactivity on the racial issue. When Sam got off the bus at Main Street a short while later, we were still quite far apart on the question.

But that evening, when I was sitting in my room trying to read, I kept thinking about what Sam had said. Maybe Sam is right about Peter and about me, too, actually, I finally conceded. Have I ever really had a Negro friend, despite my championing of their cause? I feel somewhat uncomfortable with Negro people, but I'm not supposed to admit that to myself because they're poor and oppressed and need my benevolent and enlightened assistance. I laughed sardonically. I'd felt guilty because I hadn't reacted automatically when the tough used the word "nigger." That's what really had been bothering me. I realized how little genuine thinking about things I actually did.

So I began the practice of systematically mulling things over during my long walks. Also, I started keeping a journal, my first serious attempt at writing in my own voice rather than imitating someone else's. I asked myself such questions as: Was I lacking in masculinity because I hadn't gotten involved in the fight? And did I really want to go to graduate school, or was I just trying to please my parents?

One evening my mother told me that she'd just spoken on the phone to Peter's mother. The big news was that Peter had finally acceded to his parents' pleas and agreed to see a psychologist. It sounded hopeful, but I cautiously reserved judgment, wondering whether Peter was merely trying to get his parents off his back. I refrained from calling him, though, fearing the usual awkward silences.

Several weeks later, one typically uncomfortable August afternoon, Peter paid me a visit. We hadn't seen or talked to each other in over a month, and now all of Peter's bandages were removed. He seemed quite animated, and I sensed he had something important to tell me. We had milk and cookies, chatting for a while with my mother, who had some free time until her next remedial reading pupil arrived. She sounded pleased when Peter said he was seriously considering returning to Queens in the fall. Then Peter announced that he had to go see his psychologist, and I offered to walk him to the bus. Leaving my house, we went down 59th Avenue toward Kissena Boulevard.

"So what have you been up to?" I asked him.

Peter shrugged and smiled. "I don't know. . . . Doing some thinking, I guess."

"What about?"

"Oh, you know, a lot of things. Like politics, for instance. You know, like maybe I was just like kind of hiding from reality all that time with politics. Do you know what I mean?"

I nodded, feeling a current of excitement pass through me. So finally Peter was beginning to show some insight into himself! "Yes, I think I do," I said. "We've both inherited politics from our parents, almost like a religion, I guess. . . . Not that politics is necessarily a bad thing, but when you use it as a substitute for other things. . . ."

Peter's head bobbed up and down rapidly. "Yeah, yeah, that's right, that's exactly what I mean. . . . Say, did you ever read *The Trial* by Kafka?"

"Yeah, a few years ago."

Peter's hands moved about excitedly. "O.K., good. Well, you know, in *The Trial*, K gets arrested, but like they never tell him why. But, you see, deep down he really knows."

"So why did they arrest him?" I asked.

Peter gazed at me intently. "Well, maybe he was, you know, like condemned to die because he, you know, he couldn't love. I mean like K didn't know how to love other people." Peter's mouth was trembling slightly.

I didn't say anything for a while. Finally I replied, "Really? I always thought the whole point was that K was basically innocent."

Peter shook his head. "No, K wasn't innocent. Not loving is the worst crime of all, you know."

We walked for a while in silence, turning left on Kissena Boulevard and going in the direction of Queens College. I wondered whether I was really any better off than Peter, or whether it was just that I knew how to cover up a little better. When it came down to it, whom did I really feel close to? I ran my tongue over my dry lips, then said, "Yeah, I know what you mean about K. But you shouldn't blame yourself. It's hard for a lot of people. For me, too. You've been doing some good thinking lately. We've never talked about any of these things before."

"Yeah, thanks," Peter said. "This psychologist, you know, Dr. Farber, like he and I talk about a lot of things that I never thought about before, you know. It's very interesting."

"He seems to be helping you," I remarked.

Peter nodded. There was another period of silence. We crossed the Horace Harding Expressway and now were walking along the fence that separated Queens College from the street. The campus was a jumble of squat, graceless structures surrounded by acres of grass and pavement. "Well, here it is, folks, that world-renowned academy of learning, Queens College!" I declared, waving grandly in the direction of the administration building.

Peter chuckled. "So I guess you're gonna go to graduate school pretty soon," he said.

I hesitated, then said, "I don't know. I think I've decided not to go." It was the first time I'd actually verbalized this to myself.

Peter was staring at me, his thick eyebrows raised in surprise. His eyes betrayed a small smile. "Oh yeah? Really? So what are you gonna do instead?"

I shrugged. "I'm not sure. Maybe try to become a Conscientious Objector."

"Yeah, yeah, that's a great idea. Do you think they'll approve it, though?" Peter asked.

"I don't know. I've done some stuff with the American Friends so that might give me the religious background I'd need."

We'd arrived at Jewel Avenue, and Peter's bus was headed our way. "Good luck," Peter said.

"Thanks. And good luck in your sessions with Dr. Farber." We shook hands.

"Keep in touch. Take it easy," Peter called, starting to sprint toward the bus stop. I watched his angular body move with unexpected grace, the shirttails of his white short-sleeved shirt overflowing his blue gabardine pants. A moment later he waved to me from the back seat of the receding bus. I felt cautiously encouraged. Peter seemed to be making some progress, though I was disappointed that we hadn't discussed the incident. Maybe it was still too soon.

I didn't know then that this would be the last time I'd see Peter. Several months later, when I'd just started working as an orderly in a hospital in Rochester, New York, doing my two-year stint as a C.O., I received a letter from my parents, giving me news of Peter. My mother had recently spoken to his mother. Apparently, Peter had left home about a month ago without telling anyone where he was going. Only recently, he'd written to his parents, informing them that he was O.K. and working on a ranch in Wyoming. I couldn't quite picture Peter working on a ranch, but then, probably a lot of people couldn't quite see me as an orderly in a hospital in Rochester either. I knew, though, that both of us were doing what we needed to do.

THE AFGHANISTAN SITUATION

WITH A JAUNTY STEP, I left my south campus studio
apartment shortly before one for my two o'clock date with
Natasha at the Buttercup. It was a warm, dazzling Saturday
afternoon, and my lengthy stroll promised to be a pleasur-
able one. Natasha and I hadn't seen each other in over a
month, so we had a lot of catching up to do. I was eager to
tell her of my recent successes in the field of alternative as-
tronomy and hear of hers in the field of holistic sculpture.

From Durant and Fulton, I ambled up to Telegraph, as
there was invariably something noteworthy happening on that
pulsating Berkeley thoroughfare. In front of the Hotel Carl-
ton, I was appreciatively examining a pair of beaded moccasins
made by an American Indian craftsman when a teenage boy
on a skateboard elbowed me in the ribs as he weaved by.

"Hey!" I exclaimed, turning to rebuke him. Blithely
whistling, he continued his artful sweeps and swerves, thread-
ing a path through the throng. On the back of his tee shirt,

I made out the hand-lettered slogan, *Pain Is The Path To Punk Perfection.*

"These stupid kids with their skateboards! The damn things should be outlawed!" I muttered to the craftsman, who nodded sympathetically. Caressing my wounded ribs, I continued on my way.

I was pondering this knotty subject when my attention was seized by the shrill, whirring noise of a motor. I looked up to see a man occupying a wheelchair bearing down on me. I tried to move out of the way, but it was too late. The wheelchair screeched to a halt, scraping my shins slightly.

"Hey, man, what's the matter with you? You in a fog or something?" the fellow demanded, prominent eyes smoldering at me.

"I'm sorry. I guess I was kind of slow getting out of the way," I mumbled.

He snorted, blue veins jumping out on his pale forehead. "Kind of slow! The guy's a fucking comedian. You know, you could have caused a bad accident if I hadn't put on my brake real fast. Like it's your responsibility to watch out for people in wheelchairs," he hissed, leveling an index finger at me. A small crowd had begun to gather.

"Look, I said I'm sorry," I growled, stepping around his wheelchair and hurrying away.

"Fascist! Sadistic asshole!" the disabled man shouted after me. I kept walking, pretending I hadn't heard. The guy runs into me, but he's the one yelling at me! I reflected wryly. Oh well, I'd probably be bitter, too, if I were in his shoes. Maybe he was wounded in Viet Nam.

As I approached Don Paquin's, a pale man with glasses and short hair, wearing a denim work shirt and blue jeans, thrust a newspaper in my face. "*Revolutionary Worker,* brother. Get your copy of the *Revolutionary Worker* and find out what's really going on in Afghanistan," he suggested.

"No thanks," I mumbled.

"What do you mean 'no thanks?' Are you satisfied to be brainwashed by the capitalist media, by the propaganda organs of the bourgeoisie? It's your duty, brother, to know what's really happening in Afghanistan, as well as Iran and El Salvador," he insisted, words pouring frenetically from his thin-lipped mouth, while he walked alongside me.

"Look, I told you I'm not interested. I've seen your paper, and I'm not impressed. So bug off."

"Just tell me why you're not impressed," he persisted.

"Because you're a bunch of dogmatic fools, that's why. You have one answer for everything: immediate, worldwide revolution. . . ."

He shook his head vehemently, bathing my face with a generous spray of saliva as he refuted my argument. "You distort and over-simplify our position. It doesn't sound to me as if you've read our newspaper at all. We're interested in building a vanguard revolutionary party in this country, which means developing the correct theoretical position. Of course that doesn't happen overnight, but we can't afford to waste any more time with reformist strategies. I'll give you a copy of our newspaper if you promise to read it."

"Thanks, but I'm in a hurry," I said, accelerating my pace and finally shaking him off.

"There are no individual solutions, brother. You'll discover that eventually. The world-wide contradictions of capitalism are sharpening," he called after me.

I laughed and shrugged. In front of Cody's Bookstore, a ragged-looking man who appeared as if he'd just emerged from a coal mine, accosted me. "Hey, man, could you spare seven cents? That would really help me out a lot," he croaked.

Reaching in my pocket and discovering no pennies or nickels, I handed him a dime.

His smile was beatific. "God bless you, man. That'll bring you some good karma."

I dropped a fast dime in the box of a panhandler for the Berkeley Free Clinic, then signed a petition to institute smoking and non-smoking sections in all commercial and public establishments in Berkeley. I looked at my watch. It was 20 minutes to two. If I didn't hurry, I'd be late to meet Natasha.

"Hi," a slender, dreamy-looking young woman said sweetly, giving me a radiant smile. "My name is Katherine. What's your name?"

Startled, I just stared at her for a moment. I was about to tell her my name when I noticed the nearby signboard plastered with color photos. Standing next to it was a blissful-looking young man softly strumming a guitar. Katherine was a Moonie.

"I'm sorry, but I'm in a hurry," I said.

She looked hurt. "You mean you don't have even a few minutes to be friendly? That's the trouble with the contemporary world, people are too busy to care about each other. That's why there's so much loneliness and suicide and drug addiction. You look like such a nice, interesting person. Can't you spare just a few minutes?"

"You're breaking my heart, Katherine," I mumbled and hurried away.

I strode past several spare-changers in front of Moe's Bookstore, ignoring their hoarse, muttered imprecations. At Dwight, I turned off Telegraph, figuring I'd make better time that way. As I hastened up Dwight, a divine-looking teenager in clinging tee shirt and obscenely short shorts was roller-skating toward me. Stupidly, I goggled at the words *Schlitz Malt Liquor* bobbing up and down across her chest. I was just about to essay eye contact with her when she screamed at me, "Hey, Mr., why the hell don't you watch where you're going?"

"Sorry." I lurched out of the way, narrowly averting a chest-on collision. I watched as she nonchalantly breezed down toward Telegraph, chomping on gum as she pushed an abundance of yellow hair away from her forehead. That's what I get for being a dirty old man, I reflected dejectedly, sighing.

I decided to cut through Ho Chi Minh Park to save time. My trek through the park was relatively uneventful, except for being conked on the head with a frisbee and stepping in a fresh pile of dog shit. With the aid of a tissue, however, I managed to remove about seven-eighths of it.

On Benvenue, I was immersed in thought about the difficulties of urban life when I had my first genuine collision of the day. A jogger barged into me, caromed off, and kept going, hardly breaking stride. I spun around and yelled after him, "Excuse me for being in your way."

There was no reply. Probably he hadn't even heard me. I watched the methodical weaving of his shoulders as he churned out his prescribed distance. Muttering to myself about catatonic joggers, I stumbled onward to the Buttercup. My clothes were soaked through by now, and my whole body smarted, as if I'd just played a tough game of ice-hockey.

There were no further mishaps on my journey, except for a huge, unfriendly-looking German shepherd who convinced me to hasten over to the other side of the street, and a shiny Pinto that barreled through a stop sign just as I'd started to cross, compelling me to scuttle back to the curb. "Hey, this is California, buddy, not New York," I reminded the driver. He gave me the raised finger and a few well-executed screeches as he sped away.

It was 2:30 when I got to the Buttercup. Natasha was sitting at a table, playing with her coffee cup and glancing anxiously toward the door.

"What happened, Jeff? You're usually very punctual. You look terrible," she said, as I sank into the chair across from her.

I mopped my face with a handkerchief and indulged in a gigantic sigh. Natasha looked very cool and clean, and I suppressed a momentary urge to spill coffee in her lap. Why hadn't she been banged into by a jogger and assailed by a maniac in a wheelchair?

BERKELEY RENDEZVOUS

IN *THE PROPHET,* A POPULAR BERKELEY coffee
house with Kabbalic symbols dancing over purple, candle-lit
walls, Samuel Perkoff glanced up from Nietzche's *Beyond
Good and Evil.* Samuel's heavy-lidded brown eyes dilated
like a startled cat's: a woman sat facing him at the next table.
His eyes wrestled with hers for an instant. She is apparently
a woman who doesn't flinch from life's elementary pleasures,
he decided. Samuel felt a spasm of desire in his large right
toe. Camouflaged behind his book and swirl of Turkish cig-
aret smoke, he began sending out "high energy vibrations" to
the bewitching creature he beheld so tantalizingly near. Though
she also appeared to be reading, Samuel could feel his "aura"
begin to work its effect, as her eyes flickered toward him
again and again.

Altogether, in nearly three years in Berkeley, Samuel had
slept with 99 women, though his looks were not exceptional.
With his tortoise shell glasses and dark, well-trimmed beard,

he looked like just another bright, young grad student. And despite the prodigious number of women he'd had in Berkeley, not once had he encountered a member of any of the underground women's organizations that were rumored to stalk, then assassinate the most reprehensible of Berkeley's male chauvinist element. Though Samuel sometimes ascribed his immunity to good karma, the real reason, he strongly suspected, was that these groups were merely a myth, a figment of highly inflamed, paranoid imaginations.

Once again Samuel glanced up from his book. Yes, her eyes are nakedly pleading with me now, he coolly observed, but I'll let her wait a while longer. He took a long, deliberate swallow of lukewarm cappuccino, a nonchalant pull on his cigaret, then lowered his gaze to *Beyond Good and Evil.* Falling into a wistful mood, he thought about the innumerable times he'd been deliriously in love with a new conquest, sometimes even two or three simultaneously. He saw himself as an incorrigible romantic, living for the glow that suffused his life during the first few weeks of a passionate new affair. After that, inevitably, mundane reality began its painful intrusion, and Samuel quickly became bored with the relationship. Still, in the back of his mind he harbored dark, desperate thoughts of marriage, a house in the country, bunches of bright-eyed children. Samuel sighed heavily. Who knows? he thought. Maybe the 100th one, the tempting morsel at the next table, will be the right woman. After all, I've just recently turned 30, an age to start seriously contemplating the prospects of settling down.

"May I join you?" he inquired.

"I was wondering when you'd get around to asking," she replied, her voice pleasingly deep, rather throaty.

Laughing long and loudly, Samuel rose to his feet. He gave a quick, final straightening to his burnt sienna jacket, off-white Ecuadorean cowboy shirt, and tight Levis. Bowing to the woman, he sat down opposite her, observing with approval her stylish mode of dress. She was wearing high heels, a short black skirt, and lacy white blouse. This is definitely a treat, he mused, because in Berkeley too many women dress in a slapdash, rather masculine manner. She was drinking bianco and reading a paperback copy of Wallace Stevens. An added bonus, she must be quite intelligent, too, he further noted.

"Cigaret?" He held the pack toward her.

"A man with cosmopolitan tastes, I see," she exclaimed, long elegant fingers enticing out a dark cigaret. "Yes, thank you."

"*Naturalmente, mademoiselle.*"

He lit her cigaret, then his own with a silver lighter. Then he leaned back in his chair, scrutinizing her unashamedly as he sent lazy billows of smoke in her direction. What a magnificent face! he exulted. Her bone structure is absolutely first-rate, her black, deep-set eyes riveting, her lustrous hair long, dark, and thick. A sweet, rich fragrance wafted into Samuel's nostrils. His companion was smoking her cigaret with a casual air, a small smile hovering over her face.

"You're stunning, positively stunning! You must be either an actress or a model. Or perhaps a dancer," he cried.

"I've done some of each of them," she said, smiling cagily.

"Aha, a woman of mystery, I see! Yes, I feel an irresistable urge." He seized a napkin. Frowning with fierce concentration, cigaret dangling from his lips, he began sketching in ink her face and shoulders. He happened to be in excellent form tonight. He emphasized her best features, her eyes and eyebrows, hair and cheekbones. Within several minutes he had done a flattering but extremely good likeness of her.

"*Voila!*" He handed her the napkin.

She glanced at it and smiled. "Thank you. You're very talented. You've captured my basic features in such a short time. Except, I think that possibly you've made me rather more beautiful than I am in reality."

Samuel shook his head. "Absolutely not. If anything, I failed to do you justice. Do you know that you have the finest, strongest pair of eyebrows I have ever seen on a woman? A lot of women have the merest wisps for eyebrows, but yours are fierce, lush, a veritable forest. Your whole being comes to a climax, so to speak, in the morphology of your eyebrows."

His companion shook with laughter, tears trickling down the clean angles of her flushed cheeks. "You're too much. You really are. Of course you're putting me on."

Samuel pressed his hand over his heart. "On the contrary. I've never meant anything more sincerely in my whole life. Eyebrows are no joking matter. Sometimes I think the basic division in the world is between those who are gloriously well-endowed in the eyebrow department and those who are sadly lacking. However, it's not a subject that's commonly talked about because of its obviously explosive implications. Eventually, when I have some free time, I'll write the definitive book on the subject. . . . By the way, what's your name?"

"Aquamarine."

Samuel felt his left elbow beginning to pulsate with unresolved alpha-wave tension, the right hemisphere of his brain swirling with a multitude of creative and forbidden thoughts. "Aquamarine! What a lovely name!" he declared. "You couldn't have chosen more wisely. I strongly urge you to retain that name at all costs unless, of course, you're being tortured in a South Korean prison cell and have a low threshold of pain. Aquamarine! You are the sea that we must immerse ourselves in if we are to be truly reborn. . . . And you have the dubious honor of speaking to Samuel Perkoff, free-lancer par excellence. Inventor, photographer, graphic artist, film maker, polarity massage specialist, landscape gardener, scuba diver, among other things. My card." With a flourish he withdrew a card from his wallet and handed it to her. Underneath his name and multiple skills, it read, "Your every need fulfilled. Complete satisfaction guaranteed."

She perused it and smiled. "A true renaissance man, aren't you? I didn't think they existed anymore."

"I'm the last of a dying breed," he said, breaking into his loud, staccato laugh.

She glanced at her watch, and he said quickly, "Say, would you like to make it over to my pad for a while? I have some great 1947 Beaujolais and some sublime Gustave Mahler to go with it. And if you're into Panamanian. . . ."

"Gee, I'd like to, but I really don't know. . . ."

"If you don't like Mahler, I have Stravinsky, Prokofiev, Mozart. . . ."

"It's not that. I like Mahler all right, but, you see. . . ."

Samuel smiled. "I do see. You don't know whether you can trust me."

Aquamarine shook her head impatiently. "It's just that I have to get up very early tomorrow morning. Unfortunately, I have to make a living."

Samuel's friendly features turned slightly unfriendly. Is she trying to give me the brush-off? he asked himself. "Yeah, well I'm pretty busy these days myself," he countered. "I'm kind of heavy into some landscape gardening right now. Give me your phone number, then, and maybe I'll give you a jingle in a few weeks or so."

She looked disappointed. "I hope it won't be that long, Samuel."

He yawned and shrugged.

"I'll tell you what," she said finally. "I live only three blocks away, so if you don't mind coming over to my place instead for a little while, I'll treat you to a glass of wine and some music. O.K?"

His face brightened. "Yeah, I guess that's all right."

He got up and moved to help her with her brown suede coat, but she waved him off. "It's O.K., I can do it myself."

"Oho! So I've smoked out a feminist," he said, grinning mischievously.

She shrugged, not saying anything. He watched her quickly put on her coat and zip it, then take up her black leather pocketbook. They went silently toward the door. Then they were out in the cool summer night of Telegraph Avenue, punctuated by the throb of drums. A full moon hung in the dark, streaky sky, which Samuel viewed as a favorable omen. Aquamarine had an abstracted expression, and he puzzled over her shift in mood. Probably she'll try to show me that she isn't just an easy lay, he thought. Well, I'm prepared to wait. It's always little surprises like this that make affairs especially interesting.

As they turned up Parker Street, Samuel started talking about Wallace Stevens, about the influence of the Kabbala on his middle-period poetry. Aquamarine nodded absently from time to time, as if her thoughts might be only peripherally on Wallace Stevens. Still, Samuel sustained a brisk conversational pace, producing a steady flow of puns and erudite witticisms, which several times elicited chuckles from Aquamarine.

They turned right on Hillegas Street, soon entering a brown shingle house near the corner. She flipped on lights, saying, "It looks like my roommates aren't home so we'll have the house to ourselves. . . . Excuse all this mess."

Books, clothes, tennis rackets, record albums, a guitar were scattered throughout the living room.

"You should see my place. It makes yours look like an obsessive-compulsive's dream," Samuel said.

Smiling into his eyes, she played with his beard, causing him to wince from the static electricity he felt rippling through it. "Why don't you go into my room, Samuel, and make yourself comfortable," she offered.

He bent forward to brush her left earlobe with his lips, but she darted her head just out of range. "I'm a very private person, Samuel. I reserve the bedroom for my intimate adventures," she explained, giving him a meaningful look.

"Well, I suppose I can restrain myself in the interests of sensual precedent."

Aquamarine laughed and moved elaborately toward the kitchen. Pacing back and forth in her room, Samuel shut his eyes, anticipating the rude pressure of her elegant fingers tearing at his beard, contrasted to the light, teasing sting of her lips on the bridge of his nose. A wild thought flew through Samuel's head. Tonight, after we've made love in a fierce and highly original fashion, I'll propose to her, consummating my unflagging pursuit and ultimate achievement of a goal that the vast majority of men have only fantasized about.

The earthy, vibrant sound of Greek music was pouring through the house. Samuel's eyes snapped open. Aquamarine slithered toward him, somehow managing not to spill any wine from the glasses she held aloft. "Retsina and Greek

music for my cosmopolitan friend," she announced. He felt
her smile promising him the most esoteric and bizarre delights.

"*Merci beaucoup, mademoiselle. A nous,*" he proclaimed,
clinking glasses with her. They drank, and again her eyes seem-
ed to flash him unmistakable messages.

Then he moved in to plant a kiss on her right eyebrow.
Once again her face squirmed maddeningly out of range, caus-
ing his lips to collide awkwardly with her shoulder. A good
deal of his wine spilled, trickling down his burnt sienna jacket
onto his Levis. "I see that you have a rather pronounced lik-
ing for the rougher contact sports," he observed, dabbing at
the damage with a navy-blue handkerchief.

"Be patient. I don't like to rush things. First I'd like to
put on a little performance for you."

"A performance?"

She smiled. "Let's call it a feminist striptease."

His eyes widened. "Ah! How deliciously depraved, how
enchantingly decadent that sounds! You know, I've always
thought that the striptease has been unjustly depreciated, esp-
ecially among the intelligentsia, with some notable exceptions,
of course. Actually, it's one of the most demanding art forms,
much more sophisticated than macrame, for instance, or pinoch-
le. The striptease has a long and eloquent history, which one
day will find its true Gibbon or Carlyle. . . . But on the other
hand, isn't a feminist striptease somewhat of a contradiction
in terms, a bit paradoxical to say the least?"

Aquamarine shrugged. "Well, it depends on your per-
spective, I suppose."

Samuel nodded vigorously. "Precisely. The reconcili-
ation of opposites into a higher synthesis. In essence, reality
is in the eye of the beholder, as Bishop Berkeley sagely noted
a few centuries ago. I can see that you're accustomed to
grappling with the basic philosophical issues in a most inti-
mate manner."

Flopping into a red-cushioned armchair, he lit one of his
Turkish cigarets, his lips caressing it into cool, perfect ribbons
of smoke. Then he leaned back, smiling and waiting. She
drained her wine glass and set it down by a small table by the

bed. Then, her eyes glued to his, she began undulating on high heels to the thick, sticky rhythms of the music. Slowly, very slowly, she proceeded to unbutton her blouse as she danced. Samuel's large right toe began to quiver ecstatically. "Bravo!" he called past the cigaret hanging from his lips. Aquamarine is fantastic, he told himself. Much better than Susan Cohen, who did that rather amateurish striptease for me last year. If this is what feminists are really like, then I'm all for them.

When Aquamarine had her blouse off, she threw it teasingly into his face. Despite himself, he turned an exotic shade of reddish-purple, causing her to giggle. She plucked the cigaret from his mouth, took several quick drags, then jammed it back between his lips. Meanwhile, he attempted to explore her left clavicle, but artfully she pirouetted past his throbbing fingertips.

Then she unhooked her skirt, sliding it tantalizingly down her legs. Samuel played furiously with his left earlobe, as his glasses eased precariously down his nose. Finally, Aquamarine stepped out of her skirt, making his thighs go hot and helpless. Samuel ogled her body, then blurted, "Incredible! A truly superb display of the female configuration!"

The burning sensation on his lips informed him that his cigaret was all ash. Rapidly disposing of this hindrance, he lit another cigaret and hitched up his glasses. Then he leaned back for the next installment, speculating on which item of clothing would come off now. Probably something innocuous like her jade earrings, he decided. To his surprise, with a brusque, brazen gesture Aqumarine unhooked her bra. His mouth fell open, and he nearly swallowed his cigaret. She was completely flat-chested, like a board. She stared hard into his eyes for a moment, then laughed quietly, mockingly. He felt something kick inside him. He had a sudden, disquieting intuition that he'd met this woman previously. But when? Where? He started to go through the list of flat-chested women he'd known. Though he preferred the more buxom sort, he'd also known quite a few women more modestly endowed. With intense concentration, however, he succeeded in narrowing

the prime possibilities to seven. Something buffeted him in
the face. His eyes dropped, wistfully perceiving the thick
black tresses sinking into his lap. Her reddish-brown hair was
short and curly. Immediately he whittled down the main sus-
pects to three. She writhed about for another moment, peel-
ing off false eyelashes and eyebrows. Samuel couldn't help
moaning as he gaped at the naked expanse above her eyes.

Laughing wildly, she snatched off earrings, high heels,
and panties in rapid succession, scattering them about the
room. Then she grabbed a sponge and with quick, deft strokes
proceeded to erase all traces of make-up from her face. It was
streaked with wrinkles and blotches, though incongruously
her body was rather firm and muscular. There was a pinching
sensation disturbing Samuel's right retina, an angry palpitation
in his left ventricle. His mouth hung open as he stared help-
lessly at her.

"Susan Cohen!" he blurted at last. "What the hell's the
meaning of this grotesque masquerade?"

Hands on hips, she faced him, her black eyes glittering
with icy amusement. "You aren't too bright, are you, Samuel,
despite all your big words and all the women you've had?
Good old Sammy! Still frantically chasing tail and not even
the faintest idea of what you're—"

"Aha! Now I see what you're driving at. But that's
ancient history by now, part of the primordial past. . . ."

Susan gave him a look of pure hatred. "You monster!
How blase you sound! But unfortunately, we weaker creatures
are burdened with our vivid memories. It was only last fall,
you know, and it was all so sudden. . . ."

He sighed impatiently. "Look, feelings change. Once
they're gone, what's the use of pretending?"

"Oh, dogshit! You'd found someone else who was young-
er and prettier, so. . . ."

"For God's sake, stop this feminist soap opera! It's just
that something was missing, you know, the magic, the spon-
taneity we had in the beginning. These things happen. . . ."

"For you those things seem to happen with monotonous
regularity. You weren't interested in making even the slightest

effort to work things out or talk about them. . . ."

"Usually, talking just makes things worse."

She smiled grimly. "Well, I can genuinely thank you for one thing. I'm a hell of a lot less naive now."

Samuel shrugged. "If that's the way you want to look at it. . . . O.K., ciao, sweetheart, see you around."

He was about to turn on his heel and stalk out the door when a vision swam before his eyes of Susan Cohen's splendid, spartan torso, suddenly elevated to supreme heights of provocativeness by her bitter passion. Perverse waves of desire welled up inside him, maddening his blood. Closing his eyes, he meditated, but the harder he fought it, the more intense and totalitarian his preoccupation became, as if every nerve ending in his body were crying out for Susan. With a sigh, he surrendered himself to the inevitable. "I want you," he whispered over the hammering of his heart.

A wild, shrill laugh erupted from her throat.

"I do, I really do," he insisted, moving toward her, arms outstretched, eyes shining with unquenchable ardor.

He blew her several flawless kisses, then proclaimed, "You're magnificent, *ma cheri*, a thousand times more beautiful than you ever were! You have the fierce, unbridled temperament of a gypsy. Forget about the past. It was some other incarnation. What counts is now, the ecstatic present. It would be unforgivable for us to waste it."

Swiftly he moved forward to consecrate Susan's lips with a trembling kiss. He felt himself being unceremoniously shoved away, harsh laughter slapping him in the face. Samuel clenched his fists, feeling anger stir within him. I have a good mind to take her by force, the cock teaser! he fumed.

"You're incredible, Samuel, really incredible," she said, shaking her head. "I absolutely wouldn't believe you if someone had told me about you. Your beautiful words are just empty rhetoric to me now."

He stared coldly at her, the corners of his mouth tightening. "I want you, and I'm going to have you, bitch!" he said, his voice shaking with rage.

Resolutely she returned his gaze. Her voice was controlled,

but with an edge to it. "And now I'll tell you what I want. I want you to be honest with me and with yourself for once in your life. Your selfishness and manipulative charm continually hurt women. How much longer do you intend to keep running from yourself, Samuel, leaving a trail of broken bodies and minds behind you? Till your prick falls off from exhaustion? Till you fuck yourself into the grave?"

Samuel's face turned virginally white. Only several other women have ever spoken to me before this bluntly! he raged. He scowled fiercely at her, but her eyes coolly held him, refusing to show any hint of fear. Then, swallowing hard, he dropped his eyes, staring down at the floor, fighting back tears. As if I've chosen this damned, desperate existence! he thought bitterly. Maybe I am selfish with women, but what choice do I have? The burning restlessness which drives me from woman to woman in search of perfect, eternal love and enchantment has a force that startles and frightens me. Is it my fault that my dreams are continually shattered, my tender feelings inevitably mocked? It hurt me, too, when my feelings for Susan had suddenly vanished. If only I could explain this to her!

Samuel looked up, searching her face for traces of sympathy. He saw Susan watching him dispassionately, as if he were some sort of bug under a microscope, he thought. A wave of angry weariness passed over him. The hell with her! Susan could never understand someone like me, a creature of mood and nuance who soars beyond the bounds of safety and mediocrity. Her neat little categories deny human complexity.

He said, "You know, women have hurt me, too. It's a two-way street, though you feminists always assume the man's to blame. And I've never twisted anyone's arm to jump into the sack with me either. . . ."

"Is that the best you can do, Samuel?"

He shrugged. "I'm afraid I'm not interested in confessing my sins to you. And since that seems to be your main purpose in bringing me here, I think I'd better go."

"Could you wait just a minute?"

"What for?"

"I want to show you something."

He looked at his watch. "All right, but make it quick."

As Susan went to the closet and started hurriedly to dress, Samuel glanced about her room for the first time. His eyes collided with the sad, haunted face of Rosa Luxembourg on the wall. Prints and photographs of several other women flanked her, their faces gazing sternly at Samuel, as if in judgment, he felt. Susan strode toward him, wearing blue jeans, tennis shoes, and a tee shirt with a woman clenching her fist stamped on it, and above that the red letters, F.O.P. Around her neck hung a silver medallion. Uneasily he asked, "What do those letters stand for?"

"Fuck Off Pig," she said quietly.

His high-pitched laugh sounded like someone else's. "Oh, come on! That's just an hysterical feminist version of the bogey man."

"Since you say it doesn't exist, then of course it doesn't."

"All right, all right. So what the hell do you want?" he stammered.

"You're going to be tried by a revolutionary tribunal."

His body went cold and rigid. Words refused to come to his aid. When the shock had worn off a little, though, he said, "Jesus, this stuff is getting more absurd by the minute. You can't be serious."

Susan touched the medallion to her lips. A piercing whistle ensued, and then all at once there was a clatter of footsteps on the second floor. His heart thudding thickly, Samuel started for the door. Susan intercepted him, and for a long, furious moment they scuffled, until he managed to break loose, throwing her to the floor. He bolted into the front room as a flood of women poured down the stairs. "There he is, the pig! The satyr! Hurry up! Stop him!" voices screamed.

He reached the front door several steps ahead of the first few women. He fumbled frantically with the door knob, feeling his slim advantage slipping rapidly away. He got the door open just as punches and kicks, accompanied by loud epithets, began to rain upon him. Samuel groaned as a ringing kick connected with his right shin, followed almost immediately by sharp knuckles probing his kidneys. He staggered outside, desperately attempting to shake off a multitude of blows, a swarm of angry hands grasping at him. Two or three times he narrowly managed to deflect kicks aimed at his genitals. His glasses felt cracked, and his face and body stung horribly. But like a grim, dogged fullback, he fought his way toward the street, using head, elbows, knees, shoulders, until he'd finally succeeded in freeing himself from his myriad assailants.

Then he sprinted into the night, knees pumping furiously, thick breath pouring out in convulsive spurts. The thump of pursuing footsteps, the shrill bark of voices jangled in his ears. He ran hard for blocks, not daring once to slow down or look back. It's a good thing I've kept in shape, he told himself. That horde of furies really seemed determined to tear me apart. Berkeley isn't a safe place to live anymore.

When he pulled up in front of his house on Cherry Street and Russell, there was a tormenting stitch in his left side. He gave a quick glance over his shoulder, then a longer one, both times surprised to discover emptiness and silence along Cherry Street. He allowed himself several moments to try to catch his breath, then hurriedly let himself in the front door. He had an immediate urge to urinate and rushed to the bathroom. His hands and legs were trembling violently, and he barely managed to avoid wetting his pants. As he started to wash his hands, an image from the mirror drew his attention. The wild-eyed man with the bruised, distorted face and ruined eyeglasses was a total stranger. Samuel closed his eyes and shuddered, as tears leaked silently down his numb cheeks.

THE BALLAD OF JOE HILL

*As he was about to be shot, Joe
Hill spoke his last words to his
friends and followers:*

"Don't mourn. Organize."

THE TWO YOUNG WOMEN PHOTOGRAPHED, one by
one, a long succession of men standing before the steps of the
U.C. Berkeley administration building. The more attractive of
the two, Ursulla, was Swedish. I watched her small pink ton-
gue slither sinuously over a vanilla ice cream cone, while her
bronzed, slender body was displayed to advantage by a green
minidress. She had prominent cheekbones, a small, turned-up
nose, gray, penetrating eyes, and honey-brown hair knotted
into a bun.

"Turn a little more to the right," Ursulla directed some-
one as her colleague prepared to snap his picture.

The man mugged a bit before complying, bringing laugh-
ter from the other men and a tolerant smile from Ursulla.

"You will have to get your hair cut," her clipped accent
informed the next fellow.

"You mean before I can get the job?" he asked anxiously,

as a groan went up from the rest of us. For the most part, we were a long-haired, extremely casually dressed bunch.

She held up a shapely hand gleaming with rings. "Oh, don't worry! It will be just a trim in the back. The hairdresser will take care of it. The director wants the people to look like the men of that period."

"Why did you advertise for people in Berkeley, then, if our hair is too long?" someone demanded.

"Only a few of you will need a trim. The rest are O.K.," she hastily assured us. "The director feels that in recent years Berkeley has shown the strong political spirit that he wants to put into his film. That's why we are looking for people from Berkeley."

A loud, humorous cheer greeted her last statement. It was 1971, and the U.C. Berkeley campus had been a center of militant political activity for the past decade. We were auditioning for jobs as extras in a movie about Joe Hill, the I.W.W. organizer, songwriter, and martyr, shot by a Utah firing squad in 1915.

"Phil Shapiro," Ursulla called out, and I moved to face the camera, my heart fluttering urgently, eyes narrowed against the sun's glare. I felt Ursulla's bright gaze fixed upon me and for an instant fantasized that she had fallen madly in love with me.

"Raise your chin a little," she commanded, and I promptly obeyed, feeling a bit like a chastised schoolchild.

On the back of the rapidly developed photo, I wrote my name and phone number. After everyone's picture had been taken, Ursulla informed us that those chosen would be contacted very soon. Another photographic session was scheduled here for tomorrow, and then the director would select a total of 20 extras from the two groups. In Northern California, 60 other extras were simultaneously being picked.

I walked home in a blissful daze. In my late twenties, a refugee from the East Coast and failed relationships, jobs, and political causes, I was new to Berkeley, where it seemed just about anything could happen and usually did. Even my getting into a movie about a labor hero, I thought. But as I approached

the gloomy, impersonal-looking facade of the Berkeley 'Y',
where I lived now, a sobering wave of reality passed through
me. Things like being in the movies happen to other people,
not me, I reflected. There must have been at least 25 guys
there today, and there'll surely be another mob tomorrow. I
sighed. Next week I'll have to start looking for a serious job.
My savings are getting pretty low.

Two days later, Saturday afternoon, my throbbing hand
clutched the receiver to my ear, as magic sounds danced into
it. Ursulla was briskly congratulating me on my good fortune.
In answer to my hesitant question, she informed me that the
pay would be $20 and an excellent lunch for one day's work.
I had a vision of thick, juicy roast beef sandwiches washed
down by bottles of cold, imported beer. She sounded quite
glad when I said I was definitely interested in the job, and I
hoped her reaction stemmed not entirely from business con-
siderations. I thanked her warmly, not caring at all about the
mediocre pay or the unusually early hour I'd have to get up
tomorrow. My body was tingling all over when I hung up
the phone.

At six on a foggy Sunday morning, I joined Ursulla and
her associate, Susan, plus eight other sleepy-looking extras in
a parking lot near campus. It was impossible to rent a bus to
Sonora because of the busy July 4th weekend, Ursulla explain-
ed, so the drivers would be reimbursed for their gas. The
other Berkeley extras were car-pooling from another location,
she added.

I climbed into a rather weathered-looking Volkswagen
van along with five other men. Shortly, we stopped and got
donuts and containers of coffee at Oscar's on Shattuck Avenue
before heading down University toward the freeway. Despite
the general air of sleepiness prevailing among my travelling
companions and the sporadic nature of their conversation, I
eventually discovered something about them. Lou, the black-
haired, amiable-looking driver, claimed to be an anarchist.
Harry, a pale, sharp-featured, nervous-eyed man, divulged that
he was a part-time gambler, and lanky Ted was an occasional
merchant seaman. The other two men, Randy and Mike, were

students at Cal.

After a while, I said somewhat anxiously, "You know, I haven't seen any of Biderman's films at all. I hope this one does Joe Hill justice. That's part of the reason I'm going today."

"Biderman's a damn good director," Harry responded. "Very poetic and sensitive. *Anna Lundborg* is one of the best movies I've ever seen."

Lou was shaking his head. "Yeah, but that wasn't a political flick, man. You know what Hollywood will do to Joe Hill."

"Biderman's supposed to be political, kind of a socialist," Harry said. "But anyway, whatever its politics, I bet the whole thing looks fantastic."

Lou shrugged. "Hey, what does everyone say to some righteous hash?" he asked.

There were murmurs of approval. Lou pointed to the glove compartment, and Harry opened it, taking out a large brown pipe and matches. He lit the pipe, took a few puffs, then passed it to Ted, who was sitting next to Lou.

"Oh well, it'll be a trip, anyway," Ted said after inhaling deeply several times. "It beats hanging around Berkeley and listening to Buffalo Springfield, I guess."

"Yeah, I'm dead broke so even 20 bucks will come in handy. At least I'll be able to play cards this week," Harry put in.

After a few turns at the pipe, I leaned back, not worrying any more about the film. I felt a pleasant, floating sensation, enjoying the endless miles of farmland unreeling before my eyes, the warmth of the bright sun on my skin. Finally we arrived in Sonora.

There the first stop was the barber shop. The local extras waiting their turn in line had the patient, humble look of country folk. In their old-fashioned costumes, they looked quite convincing as western Americans of 60 years ago. Two local barbers and a blonde Swedish woman, one of the movie staff, were giving haircuts. I felt my stomach tighten. Everyone, locals and Berkeleyites alike, was receiving an extremely short haircut.

"Hey, those jobs aren't exactly trims," Ted commented to his travelling companions.

"I'd call them good old military crewcuts," Lou added, and the rest of us nodded grimly.

I was still feeling the effects of the hash, and the whole situation didn't seem quite real. Meanwhile, Ursulla, in a blue minidress, was continually vanishing, then reappearing as she intermittently supervised and gave the barbers instructions. Finally Lou managed to corner her. "Hey, those haircuts look pretty short. You said they'd only be giving people trims," he protested.

"You agreed to get your hair cut," she said curtly.

Harry started to say something, but Ursulla interrupted. "You have to do what the director wants for the part," she snapped, moving past Lou.

He beckoned to the rest of us, who quickly went into a huddle. "This is a real bunch of bullshit," Ted muttered, anxiously fingering his long, dark hair. "They'll have us all looking like I.B.M. executives."

"Really," Mike seconded.

"Look, let's demand to speak to the director right now," Lou said. "We're going right to the top with this."

The rest of us nodded and voiced emphatic approval.

Ursulla hurried over. "What are you doing? You are holding everything up. We are already late."

"We want to see the director," Lou said.

"He's too busy to fool around with this nonsense."

There was a tense silence. "Well, we're not moving until we see him," I heard myself saying, my voice cracking with anger. Suddenly I felt like a real fool for having thought so much about Ursulla. I trembled slightly under the impact of her iron-gray glare.

The local extras were taking all this in impassively. Ursulla spoke in Swedish to the other woman, who laid down her scissors and hurried out. Ursulla picked up the scissors. "Come on, next!" she ordered, beckoning toward a Berkeley man who'd recently joined the line. He took several hesitant steps toward her.

Ursulla gestured impatiently. "Come on now! We don't have all day."

"No, don't do it!" Lou shouted.

"Delilah will cut it all off," Harry added, and Ursulla glowered at him.

The fellow was still wavering when a stocky, red-faced, bespectacled man came in. His imperious gestures and angry, torrential Swedish made it immediately obvious who he was. After speaking briefly to Ursulla, the director stalked out, not glancing once at any of the extras. At that moment I felt intensely aware of my own insignificance in the general scheme of things.

Ursulla turned triumphantly toward the rebels. "The director says your hair must be right for the movie, otherwise you can not be in it. Come on, you are being children," she chided, as we still hung back.

Once again we gathered together. After a short pause, Lou said, "He didn't sound too conciliatory, did he?"

"Fuck it. They can have their lousy movie. Let's all go home," Ted blurted, and the rest of us looked at him, not saying anything. I wanted to stay but hesitated to speak first.

Finally Harry said, "Well, I'm staying even if they cut all my beautiful hair off. The day's half shot, anyway, and besides I could use that $20."

"Maybe we could bargain with 'em," Lou suggested. "You know, try to get them not to take too much off." One or two others took up Lou's idea.

"Fat chance," Ted retorted. But he was outnumbered and soon gave in.

One by one, each of us warily submitted to the shears, pleading with the barber to exercise restraint. But under Ursulla's stern gaze, the barbers didn't have too much choice in the matter. I watched my companions' hair shower to the ground in abundant clumps. My own long hair was lopped off by a tall, stolid local barber, who meanwhile chatted to me about the weather. Oh well, it'll grow back eventually, I consoled myself.

After this, I went for my costume. The clothing truck, a huge van, was staffed by several miniskirted young Swedish women, cool and bored-looking, like opulent statues. I was outfitted with brown, baggy woolen pants, white linen shirt, cowboy hat, battered suit jacket, and work boots that were a size too small, with a large hole in the toe of the right one. The other shoes available were even less suitable.

Then I walked over to the Spanish-style town square, with its benches, equestrian statues, maple trees, and patches of grass. The molten, late-morning sun poured down on the square, and I was already beginning to sweat profusely. A large crowd, ranging from early teen-agers to men in their seventies, and including a sprinkling of women, milled about. The men were in work clothes, except for those who played vigilantes; the women wore long black skirts, long-sleeved white blouses, and high-buttoned black shoes with heels. There was a long wait, and people were getting a bit restless. Meanwhile, I struck up a conversation with a plain, sober-faced woman who had never heard of Joe Hill and wasn't expecially curious about who he was. She had three small children and said she was glad to earn a little extra money and be in a movie.

Finally, the director stepped to the front of the square to address the extras. Near him now stood several young Swedish actors with their arms about some of the staff women. The actor supposedly playing Joe Hill was pretty and rosy-cheeked, and I wondered whether this cherubic-looking fellow was actually going to play a tough labor organizer.

Biderman spoke in labored, heavily-accented, but clear English. He gesticulated strenuously, his face beet-red with effort. "Some of you are strikers. You are herded into the railroad cars by the vigilantes and forced to stay there for perhaps 20 hours. You are in bad shape, you are hungry, you are thirsty, you are tired, you are hot. How do you say it in English? You can't take a shit, you can't piss. . . . The vigilantes are trying to break the strike. They represent the business people of the town, and you are a threat to their interests. They are brutal toward you. They hate you. They are cruel to the women and children. . . ."

He went on in this vein, but I had stopped listening, tired of the strain of close attention in the hot, crowded square. Others, too, began shifting their feet and glancing about restlessly. After shouting instructions a while longer, the director finally concluded.

The extras boarded buses going to the filming site. I sat next to Jesse Barnes, an old man playing a vigilante, in a vest, bow tie, white shirt, black frock coat and trousers, and a top hat. He held a shot gun in his lap. I asked him if he knew much about Joe Hill. Jesse slowly shook his head. "No, I'm not sure who he was. But I think this film is a good idea because it's tryin' to tell the rich people something. You see, they're grabbin' all they can, and they won't turn any of it loose. That's what's causin' all these riots and demonstrations. Now they could save themselves a mess of trouble by givin' the poor some of it. The rich better wise up. These schools, they let these young people take dope and mess around with a bunch of women. Those kids just don't know no better. They could catch a disease. I always said one good piece is a heck of a lot better than a lot of bad ones." He chuckled.

I said something about the poor needing to organize rather than being given hand-outs by the rich. Jesse agreed and began telling me about having been a logger in Arkansas years ago and helping organize a union. In the midst of this conversation, the bus came to a sudden stop. No one seemed to know what was wrong, but finally someone from the staff explained that there was some difficulty moving the cameras, which were in the middle of the road. We were assured that it would be only a short delay. But hot, dusty air oozed turgidly in through the open windows, and people began coughing and sighing and muttering about the discomfort. After about a half an hour, the bus started up again, soon arriving at the filming site. There the landscape was flat and monotonous: a long, dusty thread of road, a winding stretch of railroad tracks, and a vast expanse of tall, parched-looking grass fading into the pale blue horizon and surrounding hills.

Many of the extras clamored for lunch. A crew of buxom

Swedish women dragged over large cartons loaded with white lunch boxes. A buzz of satisfaction came from the extras. One of the staff, a gaunt young man whose sunglasses covered most of his face, shouted, "Line up here for lunch!" Looking grimly determined, he thrust the boxes with amazing rapidity into the flood of outstretched hands.

Plopping down in the grass, I pulled open my lunch with eager anticipation. I stared incredulously at the two white bread sandwiches, one with a slice of melting cheese, the other a thin slab of fatty roast beef. A gurgle of sour laughter bubbled up inside me as I recalled my earlier fantasy of lunch. For several moments I indulged in homicidal reflections about Ursulla. Two cookies, a banana, and a small jar of macaroni salad rounded out the meal. My growling stomach urged me to eat, so I shoved one of the sandwiches into my mouth, directing myself to chew. The food formed a dry, tasteless mass in my parched throat. I watched the other extras methodically grinding away at it, some of them actually looking quite contented. Harry was distributing his half-eaten lunch to some other extras, who grabbed avidly for it. When I'd finished eating, I flushed down the sodden lump in my throat with water from the storage tanks.

There was another wait while the equipment was being set up. The sun beat down relentlessly on the frayed vegetation and powdery road. Except for a rare breeze, the air hung limp and heavy, and long lines queued up at the water tanks. Everyone seemed reduced to an animal level with the heat, the scanty water and toilet facilities, the interminable waiting. People's faces reflected discomfort, bewilderment, a lack of connection with each other.

I strolled about, carrying my cramping shoes. A local man was complaining that all the other movie companies he'd worked for were more efficient than this one. Several other local extras slouched or kneeled, swapping jokes and laughing carelessly, as if the delay didn't faze them at all. Standing by the road were some staff people and their friends, heavily made-up platinum blondes in tight outfits and with large breasts, accompanied by executive types in sporty, expensive-looking clothes. Staff women, perpetually on some errand, strode by with bare thighs and uplifted faces. Other personnel were prowling around, keeping close watch over us. The fellow with the mammoth sunglasses, big, gleaming belt buckle accentuating his pale leanness, paced back and forth, spinning his mysterious eyes in every direction. "Put out that cigaret! We told you that smoking could cause a fire," he barked at an extra.

Then a moment later the thin man was shouting to those on line, "There's very little water left. Just take half a cup."

The assistant director, a heavyset, saturnine-looking man, hurried about carrying an attache case. Remote and preoccupied, he appeared like an overburdened accountant.

A carton with layers of soda pop cans suddenly appeared. We raced to slake our thirst, grabbing greedily for the cans. Off in the distance, there was the noise of lurching train cars, the maneuvering of cameras. Hardly had we begun to drink, when the director's frantic voice was urging us toward the trains. I poured down the rest of the luke-warm soda, then put on my shoes and hurried off, glad of some activity at last.

Four purple Union Pacific cars stood on the tracks. A rocky embankment sloped from the cars to a barbed wire fence perhaps 30 feet away. Beyond the fence were several large, detached-looking black cameras. Staff people were telling some of the extras to move all the way down to the last car and to put out their cigarets. Finally we were gathered in front of the four cars.

The director stood just beyond the fence. "I want an equal number of people in each car," he insisted, and some of the extras went slowly toward the last two cars. After once again graphically reminding the strikers how badly they'd been treated, Biderman declared, "You are angry at the vigilantes who have done that to you. They have locked you up in the cars, and now they are driving you back to your homes. Keep walking back to the camp. Don't look at the cameras. And keep moving, don't look around."

He briefly surveyed the assembled extras, then yelled in his guttural English, "Take those smiles from your face! One smile could ruin the whole scene. Now, the families and couples will stay together in the same car. When you leave the car, you will try to stay together, but the vigilantes will separate you. . . . Another thing, I want the Berkeley people to split up, to go into different cars." Muffled laughter reminded me of the still-existing gap between the local extras and the Berkeleyites, even though all the men had short hair now.

"O.K., now climb into the cars," Biderman continued. "The doors will be closed. When the train stops, the doors will open, and you will come out of the cars."

I was bothered by the director's vagueness, wondering whether the strikers were actually supposed to fight with the vigilantes. The strikers hoisted themselves from rungs several feet above the ground into the cars. Those up first assisted the others. When everyone was inside, the doors were banged shut. It was pitch-black and even hotter than outside. After several long minutes, the train started up, crawling along for a short distance, then stopping with a jolt. After another wait, it began rolling back in the opposite direction, again stopping abruptly. The doors were thrown open, and there were shouts of, "Come on, everybody out!"

The drop from the car rungs onto the jagged slope did not look too inviting to me, or the other strikers either. The vigilantes stood near the doors waiting for us to descend. At first the vigilantes seemed confused; then several began yelling at us. A few brave souls took the first plunge and soon were scuffling half-heartedly with the vigilantes. I jumped, jarring my partially exposed foot against the rocks, but managing to maintain my balance. Some of the other strikers didn't fare so well. An old man was sitting down and moaning, apparently from a twisted ankle. The mother of three had caught her heels on a rock and landed on her back. Several others were also sprawled on the ground, gasping in dismay. Remembering Biderman's injunction to keep walking, I stumbled onward, feeling like a stunned survivor.

Back at the camp, we found another carton of soda pop awaiting us. Gingerly examining their bruises, the injured complained hesitantly, as if it had been their own fault for losing their balance. None of them wanted to ask for first-aid, despite the urging of the rest of us. We were savoring our soda, repeatedly declaring how we hoped we wouldn't have to jump out of the cars any more, when the staff began telling us to get ready for another take. Groans greeted these announcements.

Then two men I hadn't noticed before were loudly calling out, "All Berkeley people over here!" Swiftly, about ten of us from the Berkeley contingent gathered by the railroad tracks in the opposite direction from the four cars. The two men had their shirts off and were both big and brawny-looking, with hard white faces surrounding their sunglasses. They hastily introduced themselves as Norman and Frank.

Then Norman said, "Hey, look, people, this whole thing sucks. Like it's 3:30 now, and they told me they'd pay us $20 till five o'clock. So let's make damn sure we get paid for any time we put in after five."

"They told me $25," someone else said. A brief discussion revealed that the extras had been told all sorts of conflicting things.

"Well, anyway," Norman resumed. "Say if we start from 20 bucks, what do you think about asking for $10 more if we have to work till six o'clock?"

There were cries of assent from the rest of us. I was already impressed; Norman and Frank seemed to know what they were doing.

"What about the rest of the people?" Lou demanded. "They should get paid extra, too."

"Right on! Especially with all those rough spills they took!" Norman explained. "We wanted to see what the Berkeley people felt first. At least half of us are here so let's invite everyone else to join us now." Again there was general agreement.

"And let's ask to speak to the director," Frank added. "The rest of those jokers are just flunkies, anyway."

"Right on!" Norman seconded, amidst laughter.

"Hey, anyone interested in getting paid extra if we work after five, join us here now," Frank yelled, hands cupping his mouth.

A few local people who had been standing close by, watching curiously, came over. "We're with you on that," Pete, a tall, red-haired local man said.

"They told me it was till five, too," another local man added.

Ursulla stalked over, smiling flirtatiously at Norman. "Is there anything the matter?" she asked sweetly, trying to conceal the anger which her taut face and voice nevertheless betrayed. "It's time to go back to work now."

"We want more pay if we work after five o'clock, and we want to see the director about it now," Norman said.

"It's not five yet." She was still smiling. "You're wasting time. You're supposed to work until the scene is finished. Then we can talk about pay."

The assistant director appeared. "Here's our man!" Norman said, pointing gleefully at him. "Hey, you're the one who told me we'd get paid extra for working after five."

"I didn't say that," he said tonelessly, giving Norman a blank look. "We will talk about that at five o'clock. Now it is time to return to the trains."

"We want to talk about it now," Norman growled. "Don't give us any of that shit."

The assistant director's pasty face showed no expression. "I promise I'll speak to the director about it, but now the trains are ready," he said, puffy hand gesturing toward the cars.

Norman considered for a moment, then turned to the rest of us. "Hey, what do you say to doing another take, and then we don't do any more unless we get paid for it? This one should be finished before five, anyway." After a short discussion, the consensus was to go along with this.

"Remember, man," Norman reminded the stolid Swede. "We talk seriously about it the next time."

"Everyone meet here after the next take," Frank called out as we started to disperse.

I went toward the trains with a buoyant step, as if the hole in my tight shoe didn't exist any more. This is incredible, I thought. Who are those two dynamos? But whoever they are, let's hope this doesn't fizzle out, just like so many other promising projects. We need more of the local extras with us. I smiled at people, people I hadn't particularly noticed before, and felt the warmth of their smiles in return. I spoke to them of how important it was for all the extras to stick together now.

Then once again we were all clustered before the trains, as Biderman faced us from behind the fence, arms uplifted. "This time I want you to feel like you are real strikers," he declared. "Try to feel hungry, tired, and thirsty. You have struck, and you have lost. The men who are driving you toward your homes are taking the bread from your mouths. You hate them. . . . The job of the vigilantes is to keep the strikers moving. You don't want the strikers to mount any kind of protest. You are armed and can use the guns if you have to." His words hit the heavy air like hammer blows.

"Now I want one of the women to yell out, 'They came right into our house without knocking. The coffee was still on the kitchen table.' Now who will say this?"

The women looked down in embarrassment, but finally a middle-aged woman volunteered. Biderman drilled her a few times on her lines.

This time the scene was more convincing. The woman delivered her lines effectively, and many of the strikers and vigilantes actually fought. Several strikers beat a moaning vigilante, knocking him to the ground. The vigilante was old Jesse Barnes. Meanwhile, other vigilantes were shoving their guns roughly into strikers' chests. The strikers, in turn, threw rocks and cursed them. I gaped at all this in amazement. They're doing it for real, I reflected. As if the meeting by the tracks hadn't happened at all. We still have to win a lot of people over.

At the camp a fresh supply of soda pop lay before us. The rush for the warm liquid had just begun, when Norman and Frank in booming voices were reminding everybody of the impending meeting. Soon about 25 people, nearly twice as many as before, were gathered together, and I felt myself quivering with anticipation.

"It's past 4:30 now," Norman declared, "and we won't work any more until we get an agreement. No more messing around."

"That's absolutely right," Pete nodded. Apparently, he'd done a good job of bringing some new people to the meeting.

"Now, here's the story," Norman went on. "They hired us non-union so they wouldn't have to pay us what they're supposed to. Union scale is $30 till five o'clock and overtime pay on holidays. Also, they should be paying us extra as stunt men for jumping from railroad cars. So actually, what we're asking for, 30 bucks if we work till six, is just peanuts."

Ursulla hastened over, her small mouth prim and tight. "You are not finished yet. The director wants you to do another take," she said.

"We want to talk to him first," Frank retorted. "Like if we work after five o'clock, we feel everyone should get paid $30."

"We are a low-budget film, and we can't afford to pay you any more. That's all there is to it."

Jeers and laughter greeted her statement.

"You Berkeley people are agitators. You just want to cause trouble," she hissed, scowling at Norman and Frank.

The assistant director lumbered onto the scene. "The director says he will talk to you after the next take. So now go back to work," he commanded, giving Norman a light shove.

"Take your fucking hands off me!" Norman screamed, shaking his fist in the fellow's face. "Now look, pops, we've heard all that jazz before. We're stopping work right now." Norman whipped off his sunglasses; his flushed face was rock-hard.

The Swede's usually dull, fishlike green eyes were smoldering now, glaring murderously at Norman. Silently the two large men stood at arm's length, bodies taut, fiercely holding each other's gaze.

Then unexpectedly, Ursulla broke the stalemate. "O.K., the Berkeley people get $30 for another take," she announced.

"Hey, what about the rest of the people?" Frank demanded.

"They get $30, and they do as many takes as the director needs," she said.

Some of the local extras voiced their approval.

"We want the same pay and conditions for everyone," Pete insisted.

"The Berkeley people started earlier; they had a long drive up here," Ursulla maintained.

"They're trying to split us up. Don't fall for it!" Norman shouted.

But one of the local men said, "Gee, $30 for a few more hours, that's not bad."

"It's more than I thought we'd get," another fellow added.

A heated discussion broke out. "All right, let's go. Everything's settled now. We're paying you all $30," Ursulla yelled, beckoning urgently. The extras started hesitantly toward the trains.

"It's a sell-out. Don't go!" Frank called out, but Ursulla's offer was proving more potent than his frantic efforts. It had divided up the Berkeleyites, too.

"I'll try to talk to people and show them that it's a lousy deal," Pete said to Norman and Frank, who were nodding grimly.

This time the scene was even more violent than the previous one. I wondered whether it was because of the promised pay raise. I watched two obese Chicano women get shoved down, their gentle faces impassive as their bodies jarred against the rocky ground. Some of the men were furiously wrestling and cursing each other.

"You can get your clothes now, and you will be paid after that," Ursulla told the Berkeley extras when the action was over.

Meanwhile, staff people were unobtrusively telling the local extras to get ready for another take, pointing them toward the trains. There was a lurching noise off in the distance.

"Hey, they moved the trains so we won't know where they're doing the take, so we can't rap to our brothers and sisters," Frank shouted. He and Norman dashed off; the trains weren't visible from the camp now.

In a few minutes, though, Norman and Frank were back, breathing hard. "The bastards wouldn't let us on the damn trains," Norman related.

At the clothing van, staff women were returning our clothes to us. After getting dressed, the Berkeley extras lined up, and the assistant director silently and efficiently paid us in crisp twenties and tens from his attache case.

"They'll probably be through with the take in a few minutes," Frank said to Norman as they stood in line.

"You Berkeley people are agitators. Some of the other people have complained to us about you," Ursulla said, looking at Norman and Frank.

"Yeah, it isn't any of our business what the other people do," a stocky, bearded man in overalls said. He was one of the handful of Berkeleyites who hadn't participated in either of the meetings.

Norman gave the man a withering look. "They're our brothers," he said contemptuously.

"Yeah, man, and I don't see you turning down that extra ten bucks the rest of us fought for while you were sitting on your fat ass," Frank added.

Another turbulent discussion ensued. A lot of the Berkeley extras had lost interest in pursuing matters any further, now that they'd been paid. When everyone had received the $30, Frank whispered to the hard-core insurgents, "Hey, let's go find Biderman. I think he should hear something about the shit that's been going down."

"Right on. And I'll go look for Pete in the meantime," Norman said, starting away.

Frank, Lou, and I raced off in search of the director. Finally we spotted him riding in the back seat of a very slow-moving black Buick. Frank dashed over to him. "Mr. Biderman, we'd like to talk to you," he said breathlessly, trotting along with the car.

"Yes?" Biderman replied coldly, flashing him a rapid glance.

"Well, first of all, we think that people should get paid more than $30 if they work past six o'clock because—"

"You got more money, and you're still not satisfied," the director snapped.

"But, Mr. Biderman—"

"Troublemaker, leave me alone!" The director hastily rolled up his partially opened window. Behind the sealed window, he looked as if he were encased in a glass tomb as he sat rigid, staring stiffly ahead.

"You pig! Biderman, you fucking social-democratic pig!" Frank screamed, shooting a stream of saliva smack against the window. The director's face went chalk-white. The car shot forward, moving swiftly away.

"You scored a bulls-eye on the window, anyway," I said, laughing.

We rejoined the others, soon discovering that Biderman wanted the local extras to do a new scene at a nearby town, Burning Springs. The Berkeley people without cars at the filming site, Ursulla explained, would have to ride to Burning Springs because of the shortage of buses. Then one of the buses would take the Berkeleyites back to Sonora.

"I'm staying all the way to see that the local people don't get screwed," Norman said. Lou, I, and several others decided to stay, along with Norman and Frank.

At Burning Springs, Ursulla said, "You will have to wait until the scene is ended. There aren't enough buses." A loud groan went up from those who'd planned to be on their way home soon.

"Now we'll demand $45 for everyone," Norman said angrily.

"Do you think we can get that?" I asked.

"That's up to us. We have to keep talking to people, showing them how they're getting systematically ripped-off, that all this bullshit isn't accidental." Like a football coach, he cuffed me on the shoulder. "Come on, Phil, up and at 'em."

I grinned nervously.

In this scene, the local people were being doused by over-head hoses. The valiant strikers were suffering still another defeat at the hands of the heartless establishment, it seemed. The scene was lyrically framed by the reddish-orange glow of the setting sun.

On my bus back to Sonora, the local extras complained more freely than previously. The mother of three, her hair looking damp and tousled, said, "If I'd of known we'd go through all this, I wouldn't of come." I, along with Norman and one or two others, was speaking urgently to people, encouraging them to voice their anger. Still, though, feelings of indignation continued to be expressed in a rather muted, cautious fashion, as if people feared their hard-earned pay might be withheld if they caused any trouble.

It was dark when the buses arrived in Sonora. The local extras began lining up for their pay at both sides of a long table in front of the movie staff's motel. Norman whispered to several of us, "Let's all get in line. I'll try to get near the front. We can pull this thing off if the people stand behind us."

I felt tense but exhilarated as I stood right behind Norman. "Hey, people," Norman boomed. "We think everyone should be paid $45 because they kept us all here till dark. And also the people with lines to say should get much more than that. We can get it if we all stand together on this."

There was a hum of excitement among the extras, followed by many muffled conversations, but for the most part, people didn't commit themselves. Meanwhile, Ursulla, who was giving the Berkeley extras furious glances, had triumphantly arranged a ride home for four Berkeleyites who claimed they were too tired to stick around any longer. That left six from the Berkeley contingent.

"If those dudes try anything, I'm ready for them," Norman muttered between clenched teeth to me and Frank. "I'll turn the whole fucking table in their damn faces."

"Be careful," I advised. "We don't want them calling the cops."

"Don't worry," Frank said. "They won't call the pigs because they want to keep things cool. They're social democrats; they're sneaky. They try to buy the people off with a few concessions. They talk tough, but if you stand up to them, they crap in their pants."

The two lines began moving forward, and the first few local people were paid $30. The assistant director, the thin man, and two staff women were sitting at the table. The director was nowhere in sight. Then Norman was standing at the head of the line. The turbid, heavy-lidded eyes of the assistant director hardened with anger as Norman addressed him. "Look, pops, you're getting off easy. We want $45 for everyone and $90 for the people with lines to speak. . . . You know, we could make trouble for you if you want to be shitty about it."

The staff women's faces were frightened. But the gaunt fellow, his sunglasses off now, examined Norman with deliberate scorn. The Swede's prominent brown eyes were narrowed tautly as he hissed, "Look, this is absurd. We paid you $30, as we agreed to. So what more do you want?"

"They want to intimidate us," the assistant director growled.

"Look, man," Norman snapped, finger leveled like a stiletto at the phlegmatic-looking Swede. "We're only asking for what's ours. You screwed up with the buses so we couldn't leave earlier if we wanted to. You kept us all here till nine o'clock, and we should be paid for that. If we're not, we'll spread the word around that a flick about Joe Hill uses scab labor."

The assistant director stared right through Norman and then dropped his head in thought. Finally he looked up and sighed heavily. "We will pay these hoodlums what they ask for so they will leave us alone," he announced to his colleagues.

"Hey, we've won, everybody! We've won!" Norman yelled, throwing his powerful arms in the air. "Everybody gets $45, and the people with lines get $90."

A buzz of excitement swept through the extras. The four people sitting at the table appeared especially isolated now. They sat with heads bowed or else gazed blankly into space. Ursulla looked haggard and emaciated, almost like an old woman. We got our additional $15, and the locals received their full pay. When everybody had been paid, people came up to Norman, shaking his hand and thanking him

profusely. Meanwhile, I and the other Berkeley men were go-
ing about, talking warmly with people, laughing and shaking
hands freely.

"You boys are wonderful," the woman who was paid
$90 said.

"It was a pleasure to meet all of you," Norman shouted.

He and Pete shook hands vigorously. "I really wish I
could stick around to follow up on all this," Norman said.
"If I didn't have prior commitments in the Bay Area, I would,
man, I really would. But you'll be around, Pete, so things
are in good hands."

"Thanks," Pete grinned. "I'll do what I can. This was
really terrific. Maybe it will fire people up from now on."

"It's a start at least," Norman said.

There were final handshakes and goodbyes. The movie
staff, with glazed, weary expressions, were silently packing
things up. Frank, I, and the other Berkeleyites headed toward
Norman's car a few blocks away.

"This was incredible," I said. "Old Joe Hill must be
laughing in his grave right now."

Norman grinned. "Yeah, it was beautiful. Looking at
those bastards' sour faces there at the end made up for all the
fucking bullshit. . . .. But like this is just a beginning, of course.
Sure people are happy about getting more money, but it goes
way beyond money, man, though that's a good organizing de-
vice. The important thing is raising peoples' consciousness,
like totally across the board. I really feel shitty about helping
get something started here and then pulling out right after-
wards. But there isn't a damn thing I can do about it. The
brothers and sisters need me in Oakland and Berkeley, too."

The rest of us nodded sympathetically.

"Another thing," Frank put in. "We tried to be careful
about not completely taking over. I don't know if Norman
and I succeeded in that. It's a delicate situation, you know,
trying to be a catalyst and yet not totally controlling the
whole thing. You have to be real careful about the ego bit."

"Yeah, I know," I said, remembering my own frustrat-
ing experiences trying to be an organizer. I was surprised by

Norman and Frank's thoughtfulness. Swept up in the exhilaration and comraderie of victory, I pushed to the back of my mind the feeling that Norman and Frank did intimidate me somewhat. I wouldn't like being on the opposite side from them, I thought. It was almost as if the rest of us had just been standing around, watching them do their magic act.

"Hey, let's get some hamburgers. Let's get some real food," someone suggested, and the rest of us laughed and cheered.

As we went toward the hamburger stand, I glanced up at the myriad jumble of stars sprinkled through the blue-black sky. I thought briefly of Ursulla, smiling to myself. Well, there goes my movie career, I reflected. I guess I won't become a film star after all. I looked happily at my companions, laughter bubbling from me, as Frank did a wonderful imitation of Biderman.

THE WRITING BLOCK

ON TUESDAY MORNING, at 20 minutes past nine, Larry Rabinowitz sat down to write. Nancy Tartaglia, the woman he lived with, had left for work two hours ago; and Larry had just completed his daily pre-writing ritual, a breakfast of coffee, toast and cream cheese, followed by a lengthy meditation session. While meditating, Larry had calculated that, despite the recent termination of his unemployment benefits, his savings should allow him several more months of uninterrupted writing time, provided he lived frugally. And if he worked diligently during this period, he could probably turn out several first-rate stories. Right now, in fact, Larry felt he had a fruitful idea for a story about a writer who overcomes a horrendous writing block through extraordinary perseverance, by never losing faith in himself.

Larry frowned at the small sheaf of blank looseleaf papers neatly stacked on his desk, trying to think of a good beginning. Once he had that, he felt, the rest of the story should flow fairly easily. But after a protracted period of scowling, many deep sighs, and intermittent probings with an index finger for earwax, Larry got up to make himself a cup of coffee. The coffee seemed to help, and he began writing rapidly. After about two pages, he stopped and read over what he'd written. "Weak. Extremely trite and contrived," he muttered, crumpling up the paper and flinging it into the wastebasket.

Larry studied his fingernails for a while, then began imagining himself in bed with various women he knew. He was enjoying himself immensely, until he suddenly realized that he wasn't doing any writing. This is ridiculous! he thought, glancing at the clock. I'll masturbate now, and that should help me get focused.

But back at his desk ten minutes later, Larry stared forlornly at the blank paper, then discovered himself doodling. The coffee he made this time was unusually strong; a few tentative sentences ensued, which he promptly crossed out. He decided to try some exercises designed to combat writer's block. So for the next hour or so Larry assiduously applied himself to free-style writing and the creation of non-convergent sentences. When he turned expectantly to his story once again, however, the results were disappointing. Observing that it was already 1:30, he grimaced.

Munching on an apple, Larry paced back and forth through the living room, grimly interrogating himself. With his long, knobby body, stubbly chin, gray, motheaten sweater, unruly hair, and red-rimmed eyes, he looked like an outraged scarecrow. Larry came up with half a dozen quite cogent reasons for his unproductive writing day, but when he yawned several times in rapid succession, he decided that maybe he was just tired. Realizing that he hadn't taken a day off from writing for the past two weeks, he promised himself that tomorrow he'd totally abstain. He felt annoyed at himself for having overlooked something so obvious.

Grabbing another apple, Larry went outside, enjoying the luxury of the bright March sun. Usually by the time he was finished writing, it was late afternoon, and the sun was already waning, or else had completely vanished. He wandered in the general direction of the Berkeley hills, his mind pleasantly empty, his cramped body savoring the delicious release from its recent confinement. Everything around him appeared new and astonishing, though with a faint haze over it, as if he'd just returned from a great ordeal. But after a while, the story began to clamor for his attention. He grappled with it for several minutes, got nowhere, then thrust it aside, vowing to think no more about it today.

Larry sauntered past the Claremont Hotel, stopping briefly to admire its stately white magnificence. Then he ambled on, turning up Hazel Road, absently drinking in a panorama of tasteful, expensive houses surrounded by copious vegetation. He was examining some striking pink roses when the story intruded upon his serenity once again. Damn it! he raged. I won't let that stupid story take over my whole life. There are other things besides writing. With determined stride, he headed home, deciding to take care of some household chores he'd postponed for several days.

As he approached his apartment at Parker and Benvenue, he contemplated checking the mail and finding an acceptance letter from a publisher or magazine editor. Larry's episodic novel, *The Ex-Lax Kid*, was with an editor at a big publishing house. It was about a shy, sensitive Jewish boy growing up and finding himself through his painting in a tough Brooklyn neighborhood of the 1940s and '50s. Larry's stories about Bernie Lustig, a scholarship student who leaves home and college to become a writer, were distributed among four or five small magazines. His stomach felt hollow when he twisted open the mailbox and discovered only the telephone bill. Christ! They've all had my stuff for at least a month now, he fumed. If I don't hear from them soon, I'll have to write some letters. Dejectedly shaking his head, Larry started for the grocery.

As he shopped, he began formulating polite but firm letters to various editors. When he'd paid for his groceries and was almost home, he realized that he'd forgotten to pick up light bulbs, paper towels, and bread. Those damn editors! Why don't they ever stop and consider what we writers have to go through? he reflected bitterly.

After Larry had put the groceries away, he opened a can of Budweiser and started reading the *San Francisco Chronicle.* He found it a welcome diversion, especially the sports page. But when he came to the item divulging that Norman Mailer was getting a million dollar advance on a book he hadn't written yet, Larry slammed down the newspaper. "Damn four-flusher, that Mailer!" he growled, thinking, My writing is better than his, more honest anyway, and I'm an utter unknown, earning nothing, while he's a millionaire, a household name. Even illiterates know who Norman Mailer is.

Larry spent the rest of the afternoon cleaning up the apartment and looking forward to Nancy's coming home. He labored at eliminating every visible speck of dirt and film of dust, pretending by doing so he was rubbing out Norman Mailer. Consequently, by six o'clock Larry was feeling relatively civil again.

Nancy got home then from her job as a life-drawing model, followed by several hours work at her studio on an oil painting, a large San Francisco landscape. Though obviously tired, she chattered animatedly about the teacher, art students, various people she'd observed on the bus and in a quaint San Francisco restaurant. She was pleased with her oil painting, which was nearly finished, and had a prospective customer for one or two of her other paintings. Larry listened, silently for the most part, occasionally smiling faintly or murmuring a monosyllabic response. After noting gratefully that he'd cleaned up the apartment, Nancy asked how his day had gone.

Larry shrugged and muttered, "It was a waste. I couldn't get to first base on that damn story."

She nodded thoughtfully, then said, "You know, you've been pushing yourself awfully hard lately. I think you could use a rest."

"Yeah, I know. I'm planning to take tomorrow off."

Nancy kissed him. "Good. Now let's have a nice supper, and later this evening we'll do something that should take your mind off writing. O.K? I brought home a bottle of apricot wine especially for the occasion."

He grinned. "Fine. You've got yourself a deal."

Next morning, meditating on how to spend his day off, Larry decided that he'd probably enjoy just staying home and reading. He was usually so drained from a day's writing that he never managed to read much besides the paper any more. He settled down on the couch with Erich Remarque's *The Night In Lisbon*. Soon, though, the urge to write a lyrical, suspenseful novel dealing with cosmic themes tugged at him. He leaped up from the couch, prepared to start outling a new novel. Then he realized that he wasn't supposed to be writing today. Sighing, Larry returned to the couch and Remarque.

"Well, how was your day off?" Nancy asked late that afternoon.

"Great!" Larry exclaimed, gesturing exuberantly. "I was reading *The Night In Lisbon*. What a book! Tomorrow I'm going to start working on a serious novel instead of that silly little story."

Nancy just smiled as Larry discoursed at length on the complex, interwoven themes of his projected novel. As he talked, his enthusiasm steadily mounted, so that once again he had to restrain himself from going to his desk.

The next day Larry commenced work on his outline. At first it went well, but after a while it began bogging down. Reluctantly, he put it aside and returned to his story. Still again, he felt as if he were grappling with a phantom. Around three o'clock Larry staggered from his chair, muttering under his breath.

"I really don't know what the hell's going on!" he complained to Nancy that evening.

"Maybe you need more time off than just one day," she suggested.

Larry pondered this. "Yeah, maybe I do, but the thing is, soon I'll have to start looking for a job."

Nancy smiled wearily. "Do you want me to play the violins for you? Look, at this rate, Larry, you'll give us both a nervous breakdown. For your sake and mine, I suggest you take a couple of days off, anyway."

"Yeah, I guess you're right," he finally conceded, nodding

sheepishly.

Larry decided to take a whole week's respite to show Nancy that he was serious about seeking a solution. The first few days he filled easily with reading, long walks, listening to music, relaxed sessions with Nancy and his friends. The last two or three days were quite difficult, however, as Larry couldn't help dwelling on all the writing time he was losing. Still, as if swallowing some bitter but necessary medicine, he made himself stay idle the entire seven days.

Returning to his desk, Larry meditated, then took up his pen and stared determinedly at the loose-leaf paper. The paper impassively met his gaze; his writing block was entrenched as solidly as ever. The same old stale ideas oozed from his weary brain. "My God!" he bellowed, flinging down his pen. "What the hell am I supposed to do, take a couple of years off?"

After consulting with Nancy, who suggested a more radical break from his routine this time, Larry grudgingly consented to another week's vacation. He called up an old tennis buddy, and they spent several afternoons that week playing tennis. Despite a long lay-off, Larry found himself playing surprisingly well, hitting his groundstrokes crisply and volleying and serving strongly, too. On the days he didn't play tennis, Larry spent time in San Francisco, going to museums, movies, and restaurants. He was genuinely enjoying his week off, until the last day, when he received several large envelopes from the mailman. Along with his manuscripts, they contained two terse rejection letters from magazine editors and a long letter from the book editor, Walter Galsworthy, informing Larry that his alleged novel didn't fit into any recognizable literary genre or category and that therefore he should seriously consider rewriting it. Pompous ass! Larry raged. Galsworthy wouldn't know genuine writing if it hit him in the face. After five years work on it, I'll be damned if I rewrite the thing again. Larry's despondent mood wasn't helped by the fact that only yesterday Nancy had divulged that she'd just sold two of her paintings and had been offered a showing at a well-known San Francisco art gallery in the fall.

That evening, after much brooding, Larry said to Nancy,

"You know, maybe Galsworthy's right. Maybe it isn't really a novel. I'm probably just fooling myself about being a writer. I think I'll look into becoming a computer programmer."

Nancy glared at him. "Stop it, Larry! You can't let what one editor says destroy your self-confidence. You've written a novel and a good one, too."

So the next day Larry dutifully sat down at his desk. But his mind was silent, and waves of nausea churned through him, bringing tears to his eyes. Growling about the colossal stupidity of editors, he stood up, giving his chair a vicious kick. He fired off a rather vitriolic letter to Galsworthy, but that didn't seem to help, though, when Larry confronted his story once again. He threw up his hands. I'm definitely washed up, he mused bleakly. At the advanced age of 35, I'm finished. He consoled himself with the thought that this had happened to many talented writers through the centuries. Sitting with bowed head, he reflected that his savings were getting dangerously low. Though he complained vehemently to Nancy about having to look for a job, secretly he was relieved.

Methodically, day after day, Larry combed the streets of Berkeley, hunting for work. After several weeks he found a full-time position as a shipping clerk in a bookstore. The elation of working in a bookstore quickly wore off, though. The boss, Mr. Hobson, was nervous and tyrannical, and the work was poorly compensated, unremitting, and dull. Larry generally staggered home exhausted at five o'clock each afternoon. At night he was content to read the paper or an undemanding book, then drop off to an early and sound sleep. Occasionally, he dreamed of writing again when he'd eventually saved up enough money to quit the job. It was easier to stay at this job, he felt, than to quit now and have to look for another one all over again.

Trudging home from work one afternoon in June, Larry routinely opened the mailbox, expecting the usual assortment of bills and junk. His heart quickened. Next to the P.G.&E. bill was a letter from *Image*, a well-known small magazine that had kept his story since February. Larry ripped open the envelope, his hands trembling as he read the first line. He re-read

it two more times. Incredible! *Image* is actually taking my
story! My first published story! he exulted, feeling giddy.
He tried to read the rest of the letter, but the words kept blur-
ring, dancing crazily away from his tired eyes. Racing up the
stairs, he tripped, barely managing to avert a bad spill. Larry
paced back and forth over the apartment, waiting impatiently
for Nancy to come home. That evening they celebrated his
success with a bottle of champagne, followed by a Chinese
dinner.

At work the next day Larry's resurrected brain was flood-
ed with a multitude of ideas for his writing block story. Con-
sequently, in a blissful haze, he mailed a large shipment of
books to the wrong address. Mr. Hobson, having discovered
Larry's error later that day, railed at him, threatening to fire
Larry if he ever made a mistake like that again. Meanwhile,
Larry tried hard to look appropriately penitent, as new ideas
kept whirling non-stop through his brain. Somehow, he managed
not to make any more conspicuous mistakes the rest of the
afternoon.

That evening after supper, Larry sat down to write. The
words spilled effortlessly onto the paper. In just three hours,
he'd completed a first draft that felt almost like a final one. It
was a humorous piece about a Berkeley writer struggling with a
story about a writing block and getting nowhere. Finally, the
writer resorts to the desperate expedient of carrying on long
dialogues in his mind with famous writers. He is showered with
suggestions for his story, but unfortunately the advice is usual-
ly conflicting, and the writer becomes even more confused and
dejected. Still, over a period of months, he grimly persists with
his story though his whole life is disintegrating. Then one night
in a dream the answer unambiguously comes to him, and the
next morning he is able to write the story.

"Hey, I've finally got it!" Larry yelled, grabbing a bottle
of brandy and two glasses and dashing into the bedroom.

Nancy, who'd been drifting off to sleep, woke up with a
start. With a drowsy smile, she accepted the glass of brandy
Larry offered her, and they proceeded to celebrate the end of
his monumental writing block.

NIRVANA ON A SUMMER AFTERNOON

HIS BACK TO A WALL covered with art nouveau, Ted Bitterman sat in a Berkeley coffee house, polishing off the remains of a cheese omelet. Drops of sweat inched down his pale, domed forehead as he wolfed down yellow clumps of egg and chunks of buttered whole wheat toast. When Ted had finished eating, he brusquely ran a napkin over his tight mouth and bristling black mustache, then with a sigh, loosened his belt. A hairy slab of stomach protruded between his tee shirt and black flannel pants. Ted shifted his thick body on the mahogany bench, then swallowed the rest of his coffee. He searched the coffee house for acquaintances, but finding none, bowed his closely-cropped, bullet head and proceeded to meditate on the dialectical relationship of being-in-itself and not-being-in-itself. His brown eyes had the intent, abstracted expression of a doctor listening to a fading heartbeat. Beside him on the table in two neat piles were Sartre's *Being and Nothingness*, Heidigger's *On Time and Being*,

George Gissing's *New Grub Street, The Magic Mountain* by Thomas Mann, and the *Cantos* of Ezra Pound. Ted had read through each of these volumes at least several times but generally carried them around with him for reference purposes.

"Would you like some more coffee?" The tall, slender waitress was smiling at him, offering a nearly full coffee pot.

Ted had been pondering the intricacies of Sartre's analysis of bad faith. "What? Oh, coffee. Yes, please," he said, nodding briskly.

"Do you go to school?" he asked, eyes flickering over the waitress' supple shape as she poured his coffee.

"Not exactly, but I'm taking a few courses through Open Education."

"Such as?"

"Well, I'm taking a course in astrology and another one in the Tarot. They're both very interesting."

"I see." Ted cleared his throat and frowned.

"Have you ever had your horoscope done?"

He shook his head impatiently. "What for? I'd rather deal with things here on earth than take refuge in the stars. Astrology is merely a fuzzy-minded, adolescent form of escapism. It represents a very disturbing contemporary phenomenon, an abdication of any real mental effort. It's much easier to babble about sun signs and moon signs than to read and seriously study any real thinker, like Sartre or Heidegger, for instance."

The waitress stared at Ted for a moment. Then she laughed. "You must be an Aquarius. That's a very mental sign."

His eyes allowed her no quarter. "You're wrong. That reveals precisely how much substance the whole thing has. If you're interested, though, I could recommend some pertinent reading material on the subject of astrology and various other forms of pseudo-mysticism."

"Thanks, but I don't have much time for any extra reading. Anyway, please excuse me."

Ted observed the waitress move with professional swiftness toward the next table. Turning away and sighing, he gulped a throatful of steaming black coffee, then lit a cigaret, which he puffed urgently. He glanced at the large watch on his wrist and grimaced. It was two o'clock. He took a quick inventory of his works-in-progress: two satirical stories set in Berkeley; one poem with a newly invented stanza form and another poem creating a metalanguage synthesizing science, art, and philosophy; and a history of western philosophy designed to demolish once and for all "the reactionary school of logical positivism," along with one of its prime exponents, "that effete, overrated aristocrat, Bertrand Russell."

Crushing out his cigaret and lighting another one, Ted felt the familiar surge of homicidal fury as he thought about the publishers' continued rejection of his book of critical essays, *The Adolescent Ego, Literature and Society at the Crossroads*, a vehement attack on several counter-cultural heroes such as Herman Hesse and Jack Kerouac. Ted recalled his reference to Kerouac as a "pubescent, muddle-headed, self-indulgent ex-football player who had never learned to write a correct English sentence." Such sentiments go against the grain, and obviously the bastards are making me suffer for it, he fumed. I'm 33 already, and it's about time I had some sort of literary reputation, goddamnit!

Looking grimly determined, Ted reached into his briefcase. He pulled out one of his unfinished stories, then slid a pen from the black leather holder at his belt. Allowing his barrel chest its full potential for expansion, Ted bent to his task. Lips tautly compressed, he continued his tale of Eli Levinson, a prominent Berkeley literary figure, who his creator felt was merely a solipsistic mediocrity and slavish imitator of Jack Kerouac.

After a while, Ted glanced up from his writing, his austere eyes probing the coffee house. Though the place was fairly crowded, Ted's gaze soon settled upon one particular table, where a man and woman were engaged in intense conversation. Ted could hear only bits of it but still watched the couple intently. The man had a rather pained expression and spoke rapidly, gesticulating a lot, while the woman kept nodding and murmuring words of sympathy to him. Finally, Ted sighed impatiently and looked away. There are probably several second-rate Elis sitting here right now, he reflected, with those ingratiating smiles and frightened eyes, so urgently confiding their petty little anxieties to some woman who thinks that makes them liberated men. They all have silly putty where their cerebral cortexes should be.

The waitress came over, loading Ted's dishes onto a partially filled tray. "Is there anything else you'd like?" she asked in a detached voice.

"No thanks, just some more coffee," he replied, equally distant, but once again monitoring the rhythmically precise movement of her buttocks as she moved off hurriedly, holding aloft her tray. Feeling himself getting an erection, Ted angrily bit his lower lip. Though this particular member of the female species does happen to possess a superior rump, the quality of her intellect is decidedly inferior, he reminded himself. Communicating with her is essentially a function of the autonomic nervous system.

Ted lit another cigaret, then expelled several hard jets of smoke into the shadowed, mid-afternoon coffee house air. Glaring at his yellow legal pad, he resumed writing. He nodded and thanked the waitress but didn't look up when she poured his coffee moments later. He bolted down coffee, hardly breaking stride as he did so, moving headlong toward the concluding scene, a coffee house dialogue between Eli and an acquaintance, Hal. Ted's eyes glowed with cruel satisfaction as they watched Hal smoothly and systematically take Eli apart. Finally, Eli acknowledged defeat, and Hal made out a reading list, which Eli gratefully accepted.

Slumping against the wall, a glazed but fulfilled smile softening his puffy face, Ted looked at his watch. Ten minutes to five. Not bad, he nodded. In less than three hours, I've done the major part of an excellent first draft. Rewritten, it stands a good chance with one of the top-flight literary magazines. Wrapped in a fog of weary exhilaration, Ted stubbed out his cigaret and rose to his feet. He felt a slight sense of vertigo as he shambled to the bathroom.

Emerging moments later, Ted poured himself coffee from the steaming pot at the counter, then lumbered to his seat.

After this cup he'd be ready to leave. Blinking startled, red-rimmed eyes, Ted perceived a man at his table, nursing a cup of coffee.

"Hey, do you have a smoke, bud? I'd sure appreciate that divine tingle of coal tar and nicotine in the old blood stream," the stranger said as Ted sat down opposite him.

Sighing, Ted held out his pack of cigarets. "Much thanks, pal. Benevolence goeth not unrewarded," the man said, plucking out a cigaret.

Ted took one, too, then lit his companion's and his own. The man leaned back, half shutting his eyes, taking a long, lazy drag on his cigaret. Next he'll probably ask me for a quarter, Ted thought uneasily. Frowning intently, he studied the man, who looked oddly familiar. The rough-hewn face with its prominent cheekbones and tangle of coal-black hair tumbling over the heavily ridged forehead was quite striking. The deep-set, narrowed eyes were startingly bright and pene-trating, as smoke streamed smoothly from the wide nostrils. He wore a plaid flannel shirt, faded blue jeans, and scuffed work shoes. Maddeningly, though, he continued to elude iden-tification. Probably just some local character, Ted decided. Then a chill went through him, but he quickly collected him-self. "You know, you look uncannily like Jack Kerouac in his prime . . . but obviously you're not Kerouac . . . consider-ing that he died ten years ago. . . ."

A smile eased over the man's stubbly face. "Yeah, that's true, but I had some good karma. So now I'm a boddhisattva, man, a genuine certified dharma bum. Whooee!"

Ted laughed harshly. "Kindergarten metaphysics! Half the people in Berkeley are half-baked Buddhists. You're as much Jack Kerouac as I'm Mary Magdalen."

"Hi, Mary. Delighted to meet you." Grinning, he offered his hand, which Ted ignored.

"Look, I don't find this very amusing at all. In fact, it's rather jejune and sophomoric. . . ."

The stranger shrugged. "I'm used to skepticism. Actual-ly, it makes things a lot more interesting."

"Well, possibly you are sincere; but in any event,

Berkeley's full of impersonators like you, attempting to compensate for their own shriveled, dessicated egos, their lack of an authentic sense of self."

Ted's companion seemed amused. "Like in other words, I'm nuts? Is that a fair translation, professor?"

"I'll ignore the puerile sarcasm. You insist on debasing the level of our discourse, I see. Why don't you go over to Sproul Plaza? You'll draw huge crowds, and it'll pump some adrenalin into your ego. Now if you'll excuse me. . . ."
Ted stood up.

The man measured him carefully. "Forget about the crowds. I want you, Ted Bitterman," he said quietly.

Ted collapsed onto the bench. Swallowing hard, he stared at the stranger, then sputtered, "How do you know my name? And what the hell do you want with me, anyway?"

Smiling craftily as he sent a long, deliberate billow of smoke in Ted's direction, the stranger proceeded to remove a white flask covered with foreign script from his hip pocket. "Shall we have a little taste from the holy vessel, professor, before we get into the heavy intellectual stuff?"

"I was under the impression that Buddhist saints refrained from life's grosser manifestations such as alcohol."

"We tantric Buddhists have a healthy tolerance for what you call 'life's grosser manifestations' ."

"In any case I choose to decline your dubious generosity."

The stranger shrugged. "It's your loss, Teddy babes. You know, you looked quite peaked, like you could sure use a little bit of this ecstasy juice."

Ted allowed himself a yawn. "Well actually, I have been working extremely diligently on my writing. . . ."

"Keep up the good work, babe! Meeting a fellow member of the sacred tribe of scribblers is definitely a ceremonial occasion!"

Ted glanced about anxiously as the stranger poured whiskey into the two half-filled coffee cups. No one seemed to be paying any attention, however. Reluctantly Ted clinked cups with the man, who proclaimed, "To joy, poetry, pretty women, and Jack Daniels, but not necessarily in that order," then tossed down half his drink in one gulp. Ted took a much smaller swallow, wincing from the strength of it. The rascal is obviously trying to disarm me intellectually by getting me intoxicated, Ted reasoned.

"All right, enough of this procrastination! So how do you know who I am?" he demanded.

The fellow threw back his head, draining his cup. He sighed with pleasure and promptly poured himself another abundant shot. One thing I'll say for him: as a tippler, he's certainly in Kerouac's league, thought Ted.

The stranger replenished Ted's drink. "Drink up, Teddy babes! No civilized conversation can proceed without at least a little bit of social lubrication."

Ted took an angry, hasty swallow.

"O.K., that's a pretty fair question, Theodore," his companion finally conceded, returning the flask to his pocket. "So here's your answer. I've read your book of critical essays, and when I say critical, I do mean critical. Holy nirvana, you're one cantankerous son-of-a-bitch with that old pen!"

"Unfortunately, my book remains unpublished, so how could you possibly have read it?"

The man smiled quietly. "Let's just say we bodhisattvas get around."

Ted gulped Jack Daniels and tepid coffee, grimaced, then declared, "I take great pride in my independent critical stance. Therefore, my critical statements about Kerouac constitute an urgently needed counter-weight to the deluge of facile, sycophantic tripe conferring genius, sainthood, deity, ad nauseum on you, I mean him."

The fellow burst out laughing. "I'll win you over yet, professor. Wow, you can really sling it with the best of them, Kant, Kierkegaard, Tommy Aquinas, Casey Stengel, and me! The only problem is, being a narrow rationalist, you—"

"I happen to cogitate with my cerebral cortex, not my gonads."

"Meanwhile, your soul is withering away."

"Utter banality! Mawkish illiteracy!"

"Illiteracy, that's one of your favorite epithets against

me. But actually, I've always been a great fan of Proust and Dostoevsky."

"There's absolutely no comparison between a stylistic master like Proust and you, I mean Kerouac for God's sake! It's that damn swill you've forced on me to scramble my brains," Ted shouted, red-faced, as the man doubled over with laughter.

Dampness streaking his back and forehead, Ted watched stonily as the fellow continued to jerk back and forth, wheezing with shrill laughter. Discarding an impulse to shake the stranger roughly, Ted pounded on the table, yelling for silence. After several unsuccessful attempts to control his outbursts, the stranger finally subsided. Leveling an index finger at the man's heart, Ted hissed, "Look, you asshole, whoever you are. . . ."

This provoked fresh laughter, but Ted's withering gaze and continual table thumping eventually silenced the fellow. Ted cleared his throat to resume his discourse, but only the most trivial, nonsensical words came to his lips. Furiously bolting the rest of his drink, he struggled through repeated false starts, each time feeling himself getting hotter and damper. Finally he sat back exhausted, tears blurring his inflamed eyes. Across the table, shimmering through a wet haze, the stranger seemed to be sadly shaking his head and making vague sounds of sympathy. To Ted, this was even more humiliating than the man's laughter. Ted was about to concede defeat when suddenly everything snapped back into focus. Once again words flew like sparks from his mouth. "Your boorish tactics won't stymie me one iota. Now here's the point. You see, the world to Kerouac was just one big, muddled mass of sensations without a glimmer of commentary from the cerebral cortex. In *On the Road*, which is supposedly his masterpiece, all the man could talk about was hot-rodding about the country with a psychopath named Dean Moriarty, and an obviously infantile obsession with apple pie and ice cream."

The stranger's eyes glowed fervently. "Ah yes, apple pie and vanilla ice cream, the elixir of life, the key to nirvana! We must have some!" He signaled to the waitress.

Ted stood up. "I refuse to be party any longer to your decidedly low-brow preoccupations."

His companion eyed the approaching waitress, then leaned forward, whispering to Ted, "Hey, this sure beats the hell out of nirvana! You know, the guys up there don't even jerk off."

"You're the foulest-minded saint I've ever come across."

But Ted couldn't help shooting a quick glance at the waitress. Flushing, he felt himself getting rather painfully excited. Hastily he sat down again to conceal his trembling hands.

"Well, well, what do you know, fair-eyed child of the stars?" the fellow greeted the waitress, winking at her.

She blushed, staring at him, her eyes growing big. "Gee, you look just like Jack Kerouac!" she finally exclaimed.

"I'll tell you a little secret, babe. You have the honor of speaking to the renowned scribbler and dipsomaniac himself."

Her mouth fell open. "Really? But didn't he die a long time ago?"

"Yeah, but after I kicked the bucket, they made me a bodhisattva, you know, one of those full-time dharma bums trying to mellow things out a little on this cold, hard planet called earth."

She giggled. "Far out! Wait till I tell my friends I met Jack Kerouac's reincarnation! Say, would you mind autographing my copy of *The Subterraneans* sometime?"

"My pleasure, babe. I happen to like that one, too. . . ."

Ted snorted. "It lacks character development. A third-rate novel at best, though I wouldn't actually glorify it with the term 'novel'."

"Meet my most caustic critic, Mr. Ted Bitterman."

"We've already met," the waitress said curtly, not looking at Ted.

"Hey, Teddy babe's not a bad guy once you get past his constipated veneer."

"Look," Ted began, his face burning.

"My buddy here and I could really go for some apple pie and vanilla ice cream. . . ."

"None for me." Ted shoveled books into his briefcase.

"It's on me, Teddy babes. . . . Bring two, heavy on the apple pie. He'll change his mind," the stranger said, winking to the waitress.

Nodding and smiling, she started away.

Ted snapped his briefcase shut and stood up. There was a mounting pressure in his bladder. "Look, I don't know what your game really is, but—"

"It's simple. My job is to spread love and compassion. So just relax, man, let go. Stop thinking all the time. Hey, I'll give you some breathing exercises."

"Don't be assinine."

"You like her, don't you?"

"Who?"

"The waitress."

"Poppycock! She's not my type."

A sly grin crept over the stranger's face. "She could be." Then a serious expression replaced it. "Hey, I used to be like you, man, kind of uptight and inhibited with women, even though I was married a few times, too."

"I'm not interested in a mutual confessional."

"All right. Just take a deep breath, then, and relax your facial muscles. When she brings the pie and ice cream, smile and say something silly like, 'Gee, where did you get that beautiful bracelet?' or 'Hey, I like the way your hair looks'."

Ted restrained an urge to strike him full in the face. "If I want platitudes, I can read Norman Vincent Peale or Helen Gurley Brown. Anyway, I'm going to the bathroom."

Unsteady legs somehow carried him to his destination; there he grimly overrode the resistance of an uncooperative body. But after finally managing to coax out a steady yellow flow, for one horrible moment he lost control, drenching his pants. Grinding his teeth and cursing repeatedly, he succeeded in completing his urination without further mishap. He sprinkled water over his pants, then rinsed and dried his hands and face. Damn that scoundrel with his fatuous and unsolicited advice! Ted raged. Who the hell is he, anyway? Probably just some meglomaniacal street person, that's all. There's no need letting a nonentity like that upset one. After my pants have dried a bit, I'll walk calmly out of the bathroom and pretend the cretin doesn't exist at all. That'll certainly put him in his place.

But as he paced back and forth, Ted continued to be bothered by trembling legs, by hot lumps of nausea stuffing his gut and throat. It's incredible, he thought, a rational person losing control like this. This couldn't actually be happening to me. Then he gave a long, deep sigh. All right, so maybe that illiterate asshole is right about one thing. I do need a woman. Mundane and banal, but inescapably true. In my preoccupation with understanding the universe I've lost sight of the most basic law of all. To do my work, even to survive, I need a woman's softness and caring. I've tried to do without that for far too long, over three years actually. A disconcerting wave of tenderness swept over Ted as he thought of Carol Schwartzberg, who'd left him then, calling him unfeeling. Ted had countered caustically that the real problem was Carol's inability to think, that she was basically an hysterical, self-indulgent woman. Well, maybe I was being somewhat defensive about the whole thing, Ted reflected. There were probably two sides to it. I wonder what Carol's doing these days. Ted felt swift currents of strength flowing back into his body. The walls, the sink, the urinal took on a special clarity, as if he were seeing things for the first time. Maybe I should even thank that guy for forcing these new perceptions on me, Ted mused. Hell, I'll even do his silly breathing exercises if that will help me out of this damn rut I'm in. Ted took several deep breaths. Actually, I wouldn't mind getting to know that waitress better, he thought. I'll have to work up my nerve and ask her for a date.

With an eager, determined expression, Ted strode from the bathroom. As he approached his table, an icy feeling gripped him. He gaped at nothingness; then his head swiveled about frantically, his eyes colliding with unfamiliar faces. Is this all some bizarre sort of joke? Perhaps an inane jest perpetrated by a college fraternity? he asked himself. The man's actual presence was unmistakable. I saw him, talked to him, put up with his needling, drank his booze, goddamnit! The

waitress was a witness to all that. She should be here any
minute now with the pie and ice cream. The minutes crawled
by. "Shit, this is getting totally ridiculous!" Ted muttered.

Shrugging angrily, he hurried over to another waitress,
who was taking a pot of coffee about, offering people refills.
"Excuse me," he began, and she wheeled to face him.

Ted cleared his throat. "You see, I'm looking for a rugged-
looking fellow in a flannel shirt and blue jeans who resembles
Jack Kerouac. . . . He was sitting at my table just a short
while ago. But you see, he kind of disappeared while I was
in the bathroom. . . ."

She gave Ted a puzzled stare, then shrugged. "I'm
sorry. I've been here since two o'clock, but I haven't seen
anyone like that in here."

Ted gazed at her incredulously. "But you must have!
For God's sake, he was sitting right at my damn table, may-
be two feet away from me!"

"I thought you were sitting alone," the woman said
quietly.

"Are you accusing me of lying?" Ted demanded,
clenching his fists.

The waitress backed away. "I'm not accusing you
of anything, but you look as if you might have had a little
too much to drink. Now please excuse me."

"Just tell me where the waitress who served me is,
you know, the rather tall, thin one with long, dark hair."

"You must mean Roberta. She left for the day a
little while ago."

"Really? But she couldn't have," Ted shouted at her
departing back.

He was vaguely aware of an amused sea of faces star-
ing at him now. The throbbing sensation in his temples
signaled an imminent headache. "The hell with all of
them!" he hissed, reflecting. evidently, that phony and
the waitress left together, thinking they've put one over on
me. The puerile pair of jackanapes! It's all on such a
juvenile level it isn't worth bothering with any more.

Marching back to his table, Ted snatched up his

briefcase, paid his bill, and stormed out of the coffee house. The bright, warm, early-evening air jarred him, like a blow in the face. Tightening his mouth, savage eyes directed straight ahead, Ted trudged defiantly toward his nearby furnished room.

ADVENTURES OF A TEMPORARY

"WHAT'S THE MATTER, PHIL? You seem down,"
Eleanor said to me one gorgeous Friday morning in early May.
We were sitting at the dining room table after breakfast, but
our usual conversational sparkle was noticeably absent.

I shrugged listlessly. "Oh, I don't know, I guess I'm just
in a rut. I'm burned out as far as writing goes, and I know I
should start looking for work, but I really don't want to. With
my fantastic work background and Uncle Ronnie in office
now, it'll take me years to find a job. Besides, who wants to
work full-time, anyway!"

"Get a part-time job, then. You could try some of the
temporary agencies," she suggested. "That way you could
work as often as you like."

"But most of their jobs require typing, and I guess ten
words a minute doesn't quite make it."

"I'm sure they have some other jobs besides typing
jobs, Phil. It can't hurt to try, anyway."

I indulged in a huge sigh. "Yeah, I guess you're right," I conceded. "It's just that because of my inheritance money, I haven't worked in the past two years, and it's hard getting used to all over again. For one thing, I don't really have any presentable clothes for office jobs or applying for work. Besides, with my hair this long, the only job I could get is playing in a rock band."

Eleanor laughed. "I don't have any modeling work till Monday so I can help you this weekend," she said. "Let's go through your closet now and see what you can wear. I'm quite willing to wash and iron and sew on buttons. Also it wouldn't be a bad idea for you to go get a haircut."

"I hate barbers," I hotly retorted. "No matter what you ask them for, they always give you a crewcut."

"Well, then, go to a place that styles your hair. There's a place on Grand Avenue that advertises that for $11. That's not a bad price."

"I always feel so bourgeois getting my hair styled," I declared. But failing to discern any trace of sympathy on Eleanor's face, I quickly added, "All right, I guess that's better than looking like a Marine or a Turkish wrestler, though. Thanks for offering to help, but I don't feel I should accept because then I'd be using you. We'd be back in the old, traditional roles, wouldn't we?"

Eleanor looked exasperated. "Now if I really felt that way, you know I wouldn't have offered. You've been very helpful to me when I've needed it. Look, I love you, Phil. I want to see you feeling happy."

"So would I," I concurred, "but I don't know if it's possible in a fucked-up world like this."

"Oh, you poor boy. You're just too sensitive to have to live in the real world," she moaned.

"All right, I'll try to stop feeling sorry for myself," I snapped. "Let's get this show on the road, then."

In grim succession, I proceeded to try on a motley collection of shirts, pants, and jackets accumulated over the years. I felt like a clothing model, turning this way and that as Eleanor scrutinized me in each new item, evaluating its potential for my work wardrobe. Many of my respectable-type clothes were far past their prime. Suit jacket and shirt sleeves were inches short, pants legs and shirt fronts conspicuously stained, shirt collars and cuffs irretrievably frayed. Still, a small, hardy band of survivors was definitely salvageable. As Eleanor began the arduous task of refurbishing it, I brought my suit to the cleaners and two pairs of shoes to the shoe repair shop, then bought myself a fresh supply of socks.

Feeling a definite sense of accomplishment, I went to get a haircut. I felt as if I were entering an alien world, however, when I observed several older women lined up in chairs, a jumble of pink curlers clamped to their heads, as they gazed catatonically ahead of them. Swallowing an impulse to flee, I hung around, sitting and reading a magazine. There were two male and two female hairdressers, all appearing to be in their fifties. The male hairdressers flirted animatedly with their elderly women customers, and I felt as if I were in a social club for senior citizens. Finally, a pudgy little man beckoned to me. The barber's grave face seemed to express the weighty responsibility he carried; several errant snips of the scissors could be positively disastrous to a customer's appearance. The barber, in a soft voice and marked Italian accent, said in a tone of mild disapproval, "They don't wear their hair this long any more, you know. It's not in style."

I agreed with him, adding, "Besides, it's getting too hot for all this hair."

"You'll look like a different person afterwards," the barber promised, a complacent smile tugging at the corners of his fleshy mouth.

While he deftly gave me a haircut, the barber chatted with one or two women about his recent trip to Italy, taking a brief time-out to show them some photos he'd taken there. When he was finished cutting my hair, the barber removed the towel with a flourish and beamed at me.

"Thank you. It looks very nice," I said, staring at the clusters of wavy hair, feeling a little like a movie star. I tipped the barber liberally, then went and bought Eleanor a bottle of

Amaretto as a token of appreciation for her efforts.

When I got home, Eleanor, who was slaving away over the ironing board, stared at me. "You can forget about looking for a job," she quipped. "You look too good now. I'll be jealous."

I laughed. "Look, after all this work you're doing and all the money I'm putting out, I better get a job."

That Sunday Eleanor and I gazed into my closet, surveying with satisfaction the parade of fresh, fluffy-looking shirts draped over hangers, the impeccable-looking brown suit ready for yeoman duty, the little flotilla of shoes with their gleaming new heels. I kissed Eleanor, declaring, "If they make me an executive, I'll owe it all to you."

I spent Monday and Tuesday registering at several temporary agencies in downtown Oakland. The agencies were all rather similar, located in immaculate office cubicles and featuring attractive, personable receptionists. Their generous demeanor seemed to say, "We know you're kind of weird, not the normal, responsible citizen who stays at the same job for 20 years. But that's O.K. if you'll just play ball with us, try to blend in for a day or two, anyway."

I relaxed a little, soon realizing that I didn't really have to account for each day of my adult life on the forms I filled out the way I was expected to on most job applications. Along with the sprinkling of other applicants at each agency, I was given the inevitable test consisting of arithmetic, spelling, and clerical questions. The test was easy, and invariably I was informed that I'd done quite well. At one of the agencies, there was a short film that droned on solemnly about the many important services the agency was providing and the key role of the temporary employees as its representatives. I was told that I must always conduct myself in a manner reflecting favorably upon the agency, accomodating myself to each new work environment, especially in the matter of dress. At each agency, I was given a packet of information, two time cards, and a bunch of brochures dangling the promise of assorted bonuses before my tired eyes if I recruited new temporary employees. I was instructed to call in regularly for jobs, with the assurance that, though things were somewhat slow right now, each receptionist would do her very best to get me, Phil Shapiro, work as soon as possible in the areas of general clerical and light industrial work.

On Tuesday afternoon, I walked home from my last temporary agency with a weary yet jaunty step. I've done it once again! I told myself. I've actually gone out and looked seriously for work. And who knows, I might even get some soon. No more did I feel irrevocably apart from the army of men and women encased in the armor of their business uniforms as they marched in and out of soulless-looking office buildings. Once again I belonged to the real world, if only in a provisional way. Yet at the same time, I felt an undercurrent of melancholy and wistfulness, knowing that my leisurely, independent lifestyle of the past two years was definitely over. Like someone about to enter prison, I gazed long and hard at everything around me, Lake Merritt, ducks, sailboats, trees, grass, flowers, children, and joggers, discovering newly revealed beauty in all of them.

The next two days I called the agencies faithfully, using the same polite formula of inquiry at each place; invariably I was told there was nothing that day but to call in tomorrow, and that if anything came up, they would contact me. I was beginning to feel like one recording device speaking to another. On Thursday evening I told Eleanor, "Maybe they're just giving me a line. If none of them comes up with anything soon, I don't know how much more of this stupid calling I can take."

Eleanor smiled. "Now you know a little of what I have to go through. Be patient. I'm sure something will turn up."

On Friday morning, while I heard myself mouthing the usual incantation, the brief, awkward phrases of supplication, I was surprised to hear the receptionist at Kelly Services ask me to hold on a minute, as she might have something for me. Then, to my greater surprise, I was offered a two-month job as a coding clerk for $4.10 an hour at Robert Holland and Associates, an insurance company. The receptionist asked whether I wanted the job, and I said quickly, before she could change her mind, that yes, I definitely wanted it.

The receptionist proceeded to give me the relevant information concerning the job and told me to call if there were any problems. After I hung up the phone, I sat for a few moments trying to absorb it all. A two-month job right off the bat, that's not bad, I thought elatedly. Afterwards, I'll take some time off, maybe go on a little vacation with Eleanor. Of course, now I'll have to get used to being in harness again. And an insurance company no less. I'll definitely have to wear my suit now and look appropriately staid.

I found it hard to relax that day and waited impatiently for Eleanor to return home from work so I could break the news to her. Fortunately, on the weekend Eleanor helped me to retain a sense of humor and keep the whole thing in some sort of perspective.

Sunday night, however, I felt disconcertingly wide awake. I read for several hours, finally, around two-thirty, putting my book aside when I felt drowsiness beginning to weigh down my eyes and limbs. The alarm jarred me awake at a quarter to seven. I had trouble opening my eyes, but muttering and groaning, I managed to drag myself out of bed. To my dismay, I discovered that it was raining outside, which meant my suit might get rumpled when I walked to the bus stop.

In a leaden daze, loudly bewailing my fate, I splashed cold water over my face, rubbing and jabbing at recalcitrant eyelids. Then I made coffee for myself and Eleanor. She had to leave for work around 8:30, a half an hour after I planned to. The coffee made me feel as if my eyelids were at last beginning to come unglued, and with increased vigor I set about preparing my lunch, shaving, and getting dressed. I nicked myself a few times as I shaved, swearing violently on each harrowing occasion. Several strands of hair above my right ear refused to play dead no matter how hard I pounded away at them.

As I dressed, I growled to Eleanor, "Damn it! It would have to rain today. By the time I get to the damn office, with this butchered face of mine, I'll look like a scarecrow who's been in a barroom brawl."

"Why don't you wear those gray pants instead of your suit?" Eleanor suggested.

I considered a moment, then shook my head. "No, I better not. It's the first day, and besides, it's an insurance company, and there'll probably be all those hotshot characters in their three-piece suits. I'll wear my raincoat and pray like hell as I walk to the bus stop. If God has any bit of decency at all. . . ."

Eleanor laughed. "Relax, Phil," she counseled. "I know you're nervous because it's your first day, but I'm sure everything will be all right. Actually, it's not raining all that hard. . . . I love you." She kissed me.

I glanced at the clock. "Jesus, it's almost fifteen minutes after eight already. Where did the time go?"

"You'll still make it in time," she assured me.

I threw on my raincoat, grabbed my lunch and book, then aimed a kiss at Eleanor's lips but connected with her nose instead. I hurried out the door, striding swiftly through the gray, drizzly morning. A sudden downpour drenched me as I waited for the stop light outside the Grand Lake Theatre. "Jesus! Next I'll get run over by a truck!" I muttered.

But soon I was standing safely at the bus stop under the overpass at Grand and MacArthur, marveling that the crease in my pants was still nearly intact. The No. 12 bus arrived in a few minutes, and I boarded it, feeling a fragile sense of peace as I learned back in my seat, closing my eyes. *Now I'm doing what I'm supposed to, going to work like everyone else,* I thought. *I'm a humble and respectable citizen instead of one of those so-called weirdo writers.*

By the time the bus let me off at 19th and Webster, my pants were almost dry, and the rain had diminished to a civilized drizzle once again. I walked one long block over to 19th and Franklin and entered a pale office building dominated by rows of windows, a bland glass fortress. I took off my raincoat while checking the directory. Then I carefully placed the little folded card informing everyone that I was Phil Shapiro from Kelly Services in the lapel of my suit jacket. I headed for the elevator and the seventh floor. Robert Holland and Associates had two different offices on the seventh floor, as well as two on the ninth.

It was ten minutes to nine when I introduced myself at one of the offices. I was taken to Susan Scott. She was a plump, pleasant blonde who informed me that I would have to sign a statement respecting the confidentiality of the information I would come upon in the course of my work. I plowed through a ponderous, legal-sounding couple of paragraphs and signed it. Susan Scott showed me where to hang up my coat and where the coffee pot was, then introduced me to my supervisor, Barbara, who gave me a rather limp greeting and showed me where I'd be sitting.

I was slightly puzzled to find a white sweater draped around my chair and an unwashed coffee cup sitting on my desk. It was quite hot and stuffy, so shortly I took off my suit jacket and placed it over the white sweater. As I glanced about, several things struck me. First, I had the uneasy feeling that I was the only male in the office; it was like being the token male in a typing pool. No one seemed to be paying any special attention to me, though, and I wasn't sure whether to feel grateful or hurt.

To my surprise, I noted that a lot of the women were dressed rather casually in things like blue jeans, tee shirts, and jogging shoes. It made me feel foolish to be wearing a suit. A handsome, snappily-dressed, light-skinned black fellow came in at nine, and I felt a little relieved, as if I'd just received reinforcements. Barbara told the man, whose name was Roger, to show me what to do. There was a large stack of health questionaires sitting on a table, and Roger began instructing me how to sort them. Roger was a patient and relaxed teacher, so I quickly began getting the hang of things.

"How long have you been working here?" I asked him after a while.

"I'm a Kelly employee myself," Roger replied. "I've been here six weeks, and in another two weeks they'll probably offer me a job that lasts for about a year, until the end of this survey."

I found myself wondering whether I'd want to work a year here. "Do you intend to accept their offer?" I asked.

Roger shrugged. "I don't know, it depends. I had a

couple of interviews last week. I'm an engineering student so I'd like to find something in my field, you know, as well as something that pays a little better."

"Yeah, I guess the pay here isn't that great," I said quietly. "Am I replacing someone who just quit?"

"No, you're replacing Sharon. She just came down with hepatitis."

I shuddered. So that explained the sweater and the unwashed coffee cup. I began feeling claustrophobic. "That's funny, Kelly didn't tell me anything about that," I observed. "Hepatitis is supposed to be contagious, isn't it?"

"I don't think you need to worry," Roger told me. "But we're all uptight because, you see, we had a potluck here a couple of weeks ago, and Sharon brought a few of the dishes to it."

Various employees were discussing the situation. A tall, dark-haired woman was saying, "They told me at Kaiser that hepatitis can be transmitted through smoking the same cigaret, kissing, or eating food that someone with hepatitis prepared if they went to the bathroom and didn't wash their hands afterwards. And there's an incubation period of about a month."

"My God! That means we've all been exposed to it," a heavyset woman with glasses exclaimed.

"What should we do about it?" someone else inquired.

"Maybe we'll all have to get shots," the first woman said.

"I don't want to get a shot. It hurts," a small woman with red hair and freckles insisted.

"Yeah, but I have a wife and a bird at home, and I'm not ready to die just yet," Roger proclaimed, eliciting laughter.

A discussion ensued about the pros and cons of getting shots while I continued to apply myself to sorting health questionnaires. At about ten o'clock, I told Roger that I was going to the bathroom. "I'll go with you and wait out in the lobby," he said. "You see, there's a special code you need to know to get back inside the office."

"Really?" I felt as if I were in some sort of bad spy movie.

"Yeah, it's so no unauthorized personnel can get in here," Roger explained.

In the bathroom I urinated, then checked myself in the mirror. My face still looked a bit gory from my shaving mishaps. I wrestled briefly and unsuccessfully with the uncooperative tuft of hair springing out on my right temple. But the biggest shock was my discovery of an aperture in the seat of my pants. Luckily, it wasn't really visible unless you looked very closely. Sighing heavily and wondering how it could still be only ten o'clock, I emerged from the bathroom. Roger showed me the code by pressing in quick succession four numbers on a small keyboard right next to the door.

For the rest of the morning Roger showed me a variety of different procedures in processing the questionnaires. My supervisor, Barbara, looked as if her whole family had just died in a plane crash. I heard her mutter at one point, "Oh, I feel so spaced-out today!" She reminded me of a raccoon with the heavy ring of black makeup encircling her eyes. A vacuously pretty raccoon with deep-set blue eyes, pale skin, and bleached blonde hair. Roger seemed to be trying to flirt with her but was generally rewarded with mumbled, half-hearted replies. From time to time I gazed longingly out the window at the bay, the mountains, and the Bay Bridge. There was a remote, gray bleakness about everything that I found soothing. The rain had stopped, but downtown Oakland resembled a woman whose husband had just left her for a much younger woman.

Finally, twelve o'clock and lunch time rolled around, and I spent it at my desk, chewing on sandwiches I hardly tasted and reading a book the meaning of whose words kept eluding me. After lunch I resumed work, taking pages from a folder and inserting them into the appropriate green looseleaf binder. The employees still seemed to be undecided about what to do concerning hepatitis; but around two o'clock, the tall, dark-haired woman, Ruth, began making some phone calls and found out that the Rockridge Medical Center could give them all shots that afternoon. Robert Holland and Associates had agreed to pay for the shots and to give its employees time off to get them. So in mid-afternoon, after still further debate, a large group of people, including Roger and Barbara, trooped out of the office. I continued placing pages in the big binders, enjoying the quiet of the nearly deserted office. Around four, people began trickling back in, animatedly describing their recent adventures to those left behind.

"They said to exercise afterwards so it won't hurt so much. I'm going to jog a couple of miles this evening," one woman confided.

Roger was moaning, "God, I'm telling you, that doctor sure socked it to me! I bet you the dude was queer. He asked me to drop my drawers, you know, but the nurses didn't ask any of the girls to. That's the last time I'm ever going to that weird hospital." Everyone laughed, and a few of the women concurred that Roger had good cause for suspicion.

At supper that evening, Eleanor asked me what the job was like. "It was practically all women," I told her.

She groaned. "That's just what I wanted to hear."

"Don't worry. They were more interested in hepatitis than in me." I related the whole episode to her.

"I think it's pretty crappy that you weren't told anything," she burst out.

"Yeah, so do I. But I don't think I can catch it just from leaning against her sweater and staring at her coffee cup. I'm not exactly thrilled about the job, you know, but I guess I can stick it out for two months, anyway."

The next day Barbara strutted in, ostentatiously clutching a large bouquet of red roses. Roger asked where she'd gotten them, and she replied, "From my sweetie, Chuck." She seemed in a much better mood, talking in muted tones to some of the other women, and I couldn't quite make out what she was saying, though several times I heard the magic name Chuck being mentioned.

It's like one big soap opera, I thought. Yesterday it was hepatitis and today it's Barbara and Chuck. Probably they've made up after a knockdown dragout weekend quarrel. Barbara was more receptive to Roger's flirting today. "Hey, Kelly boy, get me a cup of coffee," she commanded. Then a little

later, "Hey, baby, I can talk cool, hip, and jive talk, too."
She snapped her fingers, imitating some of his more humorous
expressions.

Roger, in turn, milked the incident with the 'queer' doc-
tor for all it was worth. Meanwhile, the women chatted about
the relative soreness of their rear ends and what exercises
they'd done after work yesterday to diminish the pain.

I spent most of the day removing bummed labels from
sheets and pasting them onto matching pages. The day slid
by in a semi-comatose blur. About four o'clock Barbara
was standing by my desk, saying casually, as if she were
talking about the weather, "This will be your last day, Phil.
We got caught up sooner than we expected."

I just looked at her. The old familiar numbness and
anguish whenever I'd been fired from a job in the past took
hold of me once again. Had I made some serious errors
they hadn't told me about? Or had I perhaps been too
much of a loner? "You mean you're not satisfied with
my work?" I managed to say at last.

Barbara shook her head. "Your work was satisfactory,
Phil. It's just that we don't have as much of a backlog as
we thought we did; our budget is tight; we can't afford to
hire another temporary for a two-month period."

It was like one computer talking to another. I sighed.
"I'll have to call my supervisor at Kelly and tell her the job
is ending today," I said, trying not to sound angry. Probably
some honcho reading a computer on the ninth floor made
the decision, anyway, I reflected.

The Kelly supervisor, Connie, sounded quite casual, too.
"These things happen sometimes, Phil," she explained.
"Don't worry about it. I know you're a little upset because
you expected to work for two months, but we'll try to get
you something else as soon as possible. Get your time card
filled out and signed and then mail it to us. You don't have
to wait till Friday to mail it."

After hanging up the phone, I thought sardonically,
when they say temporary, they really mean temporary. As
I pasted labels for the last hour, a feeling of freedom and

relief began to replace my previous sense of hurt. I didn't really want to work in this absurd place for two months, anyway, I reflected. Now I can take a few days off to breathe before my next job.

At five o'clock I went to the bathroom and waited there until the crowds jamming the lobby were gone. Then I rode down in the elevator in splendid isolation, grinning wearily and humming in my usual tuneless fashion. The sun was out, Oakland looked happy again, and I sauntered home, feeling more at peace with myself than I'd felt in weeks.

The following two selections are Chapters III and XVI from Ralph Dranow's novel, *The Boric Acid Kid.*

GRANDMA ANNA

ALL GRANDMA ANNA EVER WANTED them to do was play Chinese checkers with her, but that got boring after awhile because Grandma wasn't such a hot player, and neither was Ida. Grandma never wanted to let them go outside because she was scared something might happen to them. But this afternoon, though it was chilly and looked like it might rain, they'd pestered her until she'd finally agreed to go with them for a walk, just a short one. When they were all putting their coats on, Freddy pulled Ida aside and whispered, "Hey, let's hide from Grandma in the yard! She'll never find us there."

Ida giggled. "Yeah, let's hide from her."

They held in their laughter as they went to the door. Grandma didn't seem to suspect anything. In the hallway he touched Ida's arm; they bolted, dashing out the door and into the yard. They raced along the cement driveway, and Freddy pointed toward the large oak tree in the middle of the yard. Ida nodded. A brisk wind was in the air and made the various piles of leaves and acorns on the grass and driveway crackle and whirl about. Their bodies quivering with soft, delicious laughter, Freddy and Ida nestled snugly behind the oak's thick trunk. Ida jammed an acorn into her pocket; she liked to make things out of acorns.

Cautiously, Freddy peeped out; his stomach knotted with laughter. Grandma was rolling slowly along the driveway like a small barrel; she took careful steps as if it were pitch dark outside. Her long gray hair flowed in soft, silky waves down her back, almost to her waist. That was what he loved most about Grandma, her beautiful hair. She was plain and full of wrinkles, but her hair was like that of the beautiful princesses in fairy tales, long and shiny and probably nice to run your fingers over. Grandpa must have looked at Grandma's hair and decided right then and there that he wanted to marry her. Grandpa was smarter than Grandma; he didn't get all excited over silly things the way she did, so it must have been her hair he liked.

Grandma's voice trembled like a small child's. "Sweethearts, where are you? Please come out, I beg you."

Tiny jerks of laughter scratched his throat. Ida started to laugh, a little hoarsely. He pressed his hand over her mouth. "Shhh!"

"Hey, stop it, that hurts!" Her mouth twisted free from his palm; her face felt warm against his cold fingers. He wasn't wearing any gloves, just his favorite red and gray mackinaw. Ida's mittens dangled from the sleeves of her brown flannel coat. Her pink, round face was like a grapefruit squeezed inside the blue corduroy cap tied under her chin.

"Sweethearts, Grandma's worried for you. Why you should want to run away from me? Tell me, what I did to you?" She spread her arms wide, as if appealing to Freddy and Ida to snuggle up against her old but sturdy black cloth coat. Her stubby fingers gripped her black plastic pocketbook.

The mastiff from the corner house began to bark. His name was Rex. He was tall, lean, and smooth, with hard eyes and a black snout that twitched menacingly whenever Freddy went by. Rex's huge teeth would probably feel like nails driven into your skin. But no, Freddy would fool Rex and pretend not to be afraid. People were smarter than animals. If Rex was so smart, then why didn't he know how to read? Ida pressed her soft, shivering body closer to her brother's. She was nice sometimes, even though she wasn't as good as a friend his own age. Yes, he was her big brother so he'd have to protect her if Rex came bothering them.

"*Oi*, listen! Did you hear that? What if he should come over here? Then you'll wish you listened to Grandma. So come, come out quick before the dog comes," Grandma pleaded.

If the dog came, Freddy would protect Grandma from the dog, too. Then the news would get around about how he wasn't afraid of dogs or anything, and all the kids in the neighborhood would want to be his friend. Sarah would buy him a new Phil Rizzuto baseball glove for saving Ida and Grandma. He'd become such a great shortstop that he'd always be picked first in the choose-up games.

The dog's harsh noises had stopped, but Grandma kept on. "Come, Freddy and Ida, and Grandma will give you something nice to eat. Come, be good children. Grandma's worried for you."

"Does she have any candy?" Ida whispered, starting to take the acorn from her pocket, but he frowned, so she stopped.

"Ah, all you ever think about is candy. I bet she doesn't have any."

"How do you know, Freddy? And if we don't come out now, she's gonna tell Ma we were bad."

He shrugged, putting a finger to his lips. Why shouldn't they play a trick on Grandma? She was the worst hide-and-go-seek player ever, even worse than Ida. And besides that,

Grandma was always making up stories to trick him. Last
year, when he'd stolen that package of gum from the A&P,
Grandma had said that the manager would beat Freddy black
and blue if he didn't return the gum. Each piece of gum had
felt like a gag forced into his dry, sour mouth; he'd waited
with pounding heart for the manager to come knocking at
the door at any moment. Freddy had ended up giving away
most of the gum. He'd even wondered whether Grandma
would go tell the manager on him, but luckily she hadn't
done that.

Again he peered out. The thin, straight lines on Grand-
ma's forehead looked carefully carved by a knife. Her whole
body sighed, and her mouth released little puffs of smoke,
each vanishing behind the previous one in the cool twilight.
Her hands clutched at her hair. "Why they should do this
to me?" she demanded tearfully.

"Listen to me, darlings, I want you should listen to me,"
she called out. "This is no time to play. What if Ivan should
come outside? He'll be angry. He's drunk, he's always drunk."
She made a loud exclamation of disgust, spitting upon the
carpet of whirling leaves.

It was another of Grandma's tricks, of course. Ivan was
the 40-year-old drunkard who lived in the basement, the Russ-
ian with a face redder than the house. The sudden roar of his
snarling, phlegmy voice was enough to stop your heart from
beating. When he was in a bad mood, which was most of the
time, he would damn the children and their playful noise to
hell, pounding on the frosted glass door with his huge hands
until it felt as if the whole house were rocking from side to
side. It was lucky Sarah was usually able to calm him down
and make him go away.

"Do you want to start up with a *mishugener*, with a
hoodlum like that? He'll want to beat us. So come, darlings,
come inside the house; there he can't do nothing to us."

Ida trembled, her bright eyes clouding with tears. A thin
stream trickled from her right nostril; her breath came in
quick spurts. "Don't cry," he whispered, grasping her cold
hand. "She's just making that up about Ivan. He won't come

out here."

Ida spun her head back and forth. "No, she isn't. Remember the time when Ivan almost caught you?"

"Ah, I was way down the block, and he was still by the house."

"But you were scared, Freddy, weren't you?"

"No, I wasn't. I'm a million times faster than him, that big hippo. If he comes out here, he'll fall flat on his face chasing me."

Ida giggled. She pressed her hands trustingly against the arms of his mackinaw; he liked that. Let Rex and Ivan come out together. Big deal! Freddy would take off like Phil Rizzuto stealing second base, and then drunken Ivan would stumble over Rex, and the dog would bite that jerk. Meanwhile, Grandma and Ida would escape inside the house, and the whole neighborhood would hear how Freddy had run circles around the two monsters. No more would he be the last one chosen in the sandlot baseball games!

"Freddy and Ida, I will count to ten. Then Grandma will go inside . . . 1, 2, 3. . . ."

"I'm coming out," Ida whispered.

"Scaredy cat! This is the last time I ever play hide-and-go-seek with you."

Ida stuck out her tongue. She stumbled to her feet, crunching the leaves and acorns. He stood up, too, sighing. Grandma gasped; her eyes, small and alive behind her glasses, drank them both in. Her pale face flooded with color, and she laughed as if Ivan and the dog were both a million miles away. She swung Ida back and forth. "Ida, darling, my special grandchild, promise me you'll never hide from Grandma again," she sang out.

His head burned. He squeezed the pimples swelling the hard lines of his thin face. "Where's Ivan? You lied, Grandma. You made believe Ivan was coming out."

Grandma clicked her tongue and shook her head, indicating that he shouldn't touch his face. She pulled Freddy toward her. "Don't be angry, Freddy. Maybe he'll come out right now, that *mishugener*." Freddy recalled Sarah once

telling him of how a long time ago in Russia, drunken men
like Ivan used to kill Jews, even women and children. But
this was America. Besides, Ivan was probably getting drunk
in a bar right now. Grandma was just an old fraidy cat.

Grandma's fingers would and unwound in his, as if she
were playing a song on the piano for him. "Freddy's my
grandson, my oldest grandchild. My oldest grandchild will
do wonderful things; he will be a good, smart, handsome
man."

Freddy stared at her wide-eyed, wrinkled face, stifling
an urge to laugh. She wasn't pretty; she didn't look as nice
as his other grandmother, Molly, who always dressed up and
wore makeup. Grandma Anna had nice hair, though. He
reached for it, stroking and pulling at its smooth grayness.
But it was stiff and brittle against his fingers. He reached
further, searching for its softness.

"Please, Freddy, why are you doing this to Grandma's
hair?" she demanded, yanking her head; stubbornly he clung
to her. Suddenly the long, silky waves were falling down. He
started back, speechless. It couldn't be! How could some-
one's hair fall off? Did older people's hair fall off if you
pulled too hard at it? But then you should be able to glue
it back on their heads, shouldn't you?

The thin carpet of white hair was like a beanie over
Grandma's bloodless face. Her eyes were large and wild; her
hands flew to her scalp. Freddy laughed, a laugh that squeez-
ed painfully against his chest. "Can you put your hair back
on, Grandma?" he asked.

Grandma shrugged. "Of course, you silly boy. It's a
wig. . . . But why're you so mean to Grandma? What I did
to you?"

Greatly relieved, he bent to pick up the wig. He should
have known it was a wig, but no one had ever told him Grand-
ma wore one. "Here, Grandma, I'll help you put it back on."

She shook her head, pulling the wig from his hands.
"No, give it here."

Ida blurted, "How come you wear somebody else's hair,
Grandma? Whose hair is that?"

Grandma sighed. "What's the crime that I should wear a wig? Does it hurt someone? Grandma's old; she don't have much hair left, so she wears a wig."

"It's pretty, Grandma. I like it," Ida said.

Freddy stared at Grandma's crewcut. So Grandma didn't have hair like a princess after all. The wig was just another one of Grandma's tricks. Grandpa never should have married her. Sarah said that Grandpa read a lot of books and had done all kinds of exciting things trying to change the bad government in Russia a long time ago, and the one in this country, too. Grandpa was smart, and he wasn't afraid of anything. But Grandma, she had to sound out words with her lips like a little kid when she read the newspaper, and she could hardly speak English, though she'd lived in America for a long time.

Freddy turned away from Grandma and Ida toward the park wall, with all its different kinds of rocks like a kaleidoscope. Over the wall the bright autumn leaves of maples and elms shook in the wind. The fat, black clouds quivered, sending out a long roll of thunder. Freddy started; they'd better get inside the house before it began raining. But Ida was whining and tugging at the arm of Grandma's coat. Sighing, Grandma took out a black cloth change purse from her pocketbook. She made a clicking sound with her tongue. "We should go inside so we won't get soaking wet," she said.

"Can I have the money first, Grandma?" Ida pleaded.

"All right, all right, sweetheart," Grandma sighed again. She counted out five pennies into Ida's palm. He stared at the driveway, pretending he didn't care that Grandma was going to punish him by giving only Ida some money.

When he looked up, he was surprised to see Grandma's eyes peering into his. She counted five pennies into his hand also. He should give her the money back, but there was a hot, choking feeling in his throat; the coins felt glued to his palm. Five cents was a lot of money. Why was Grandma being nice to him after all he'd done to her? Grandma's voice was fresh and cheerful. "Why should Grandma be mad? Her grandchildren are still her grandchildren. . . . So buy gum, candy, whatever you wish. Now we'll go inside the house before it rains. We'll have a graham cracker, just one, before Mommy comes home, a graham cracker with cream cheese on top. *Oi yoi yoi*, that's food fit for a king! That's what I used to give your Mommy on special days when she was a little girl, and oh how happy that made her! Your Mommy was so skinny. She was always hungry."

Freddy's body felt hot. Grandma was always blabbing, saying silly things about how they'd all starved back in the old days. If that was true, why was Grandma so chubby? She made up stories about everything. His heart pounded; he tossed the pennies into the air. They rained down with small, clinking sounds over the driveway. Then, laughing wildly, he ran out of the yard. He'd probably get punished later, but still, it served Grandma right. She called after him in a startled voice, "Why, Freddy, what I did to you?"

As he reached the street, a long roar of thunder ripped through the sky; he stopped short, as if he'd been shot. Cold, thin bullets of rain flew down, stinging him on the head and face, bouncing off the sidewalk. He rocked from side to side, staring helplessly at the rain. He couldn't stay outside now, and inside he'd have to face both Grandma and Sarah because Sarah would be home soon, and Grandma would tell her what he'd done. Sarah would yell at him and maybe not let him watch the wrestling matches on T.V. tonight. Grandma must be kneeling down now, trying to pick up the pennies in the rain. Five cents was a lot of money to Grandma. Sometimes he'd seen her argue bitterly with storekeepers over a few pennies. He turned around and began walking back into the yard. Grandma and Ida were peering down, searching the driveway. The rain beat down upon Grandma's neat, white head. "Wait a minute, Grandma! I'll help you find it," he called to her.

MICKEY

PAUL BOUGHT A COPY of *The New York Times* at the newsstand underneath the subway. Then he and Freddy climbed the long flight of stairs, and Paul bought four subway tokens from the man behind the jail bars of the token booth. Freddy twisted through the clicking arms of the turnstile, Mickey Mantle, the Yankees' switch-hitting slugger, speeding home with the winning run!

On the crowded subway platform, his manila work folder tucked under his arm, Paul carefully folded the paper to the sports page for Freddy. Freddy's heart quickened. He and his father were going to the Bronx County Courthouse, where Paul worked; but then afterwards they were going to the ball game, a real one, not just one on T.V. or the radio.

"I hope the game doesn't get rained out," Freddy said, glancing anxiously at the thick white clouds pasted onto the early morning sky.

"I don't think it will, Freddy. The radio said there's

only about a ten percent chance of rain today."

"Goody-goody gumdrops," Freddy told himself, so Paul wouldn't hear him saying that silly kids' thing.

The White Plains Road train chugged in. They scrambled onto two hard yellow seats just ahead of some other passengers. The train made a loud, harsh noise as it gathered up speed leaving the Allerton Avenue station. People sat across from each other in long rows, some burying their heads in newspapers. Others dozed or glanced absently at the floor or the scenery sliding past outside. Freddy felt sorry for all these people, with their sleep-lined faces, going to work today while he and Paul were going to the ball game later. It wasn't polite to stare, so Freddy contented himself with a few quick peeks at people. Paul, with his black-framed reading glasses, was frowning at the front page of the *Times.* Occasionally his thick hand would brush rapidly over his freshly shaven chin or the tight line of his mouth, and he'd cough. Many of the passengers were reading the *New York Daily News*, their eyes inches from a picture of a man lying on the ground with his head split open. Freddy shuddered. He was proud his father was reading the *Times*, which was for smart people, even though it was on the bosses' side. Probably Mickey Mantle read the *News*; you didn't have to be too smart to be a ballplayer. But someday things would be different, and even ballplayers would read good books and the *Times* and the *Daily Worker* instead of the *News.*

Freddy glanced at the sports page, but then the train began to rock, going through a dark tunnel; dim lights came on, and the batting averages and box scores started to blur. He closed his eyes, his body swaying to the harsh rhythm of the train. He'd give twenty baseball cards if the Yanks won today, and Mickey hit a home run, too. Every time Mick took that mighty swing, Freddy's heart thumped, waiting for the ball to take off like a rocket. Maybe some day Mickey would break Babe Ruth's record of 60 homers in a season.

Paul was tapping Freddy on the shoulder; his eyes snapped open. The train was out in daylight again. "We get off the next stop, Freddy," Paul said, carefully folding both sections of the newspaper.

Freddy nodded, feeling the blood beat against his temples. The train didn't seem as if it would ever stop, but finally it did. Freddy followed his father onto the platform and then down the stairs. They walked across the wide, traffic-filled Grand Concourse. The sun peeked through the clouds, and just a few magic blocks away Freddy could see bright flags on top of the high castle walls of Yankee Stadium. The Bronx County Courthouse was a large white building with a lot of steps, some writing printed high in front, and a drawing of a blindfolded woman carrying a large rod with a scale dangling from each end.

"Who's that? Why does she have her eyes covered?" Freddy asked, starting up the steps.

"That's the Scales of Justice, Freddy. She's blindfolded because justice is supposed to be blind and not play any favorites."

Freddy gave Paul a knowing smile. "But that's not really true, is it?"

Paul shook his head. "Of course not. In this country, justice is on the side of the rich."

In the long hallway, people, including several policemen, went busily in all directions. Freddy hoped the policemen didn't know his father wasn't really on the side of the rich, even though he worked in the courthouse.

"You can try the puzzle in the *Times* if you like," Paul suggested. "It's pretty tough, but let's see how much of it you can get. I'll tell you what: I'll give you a quarter if you do half of it."

"Oh, yeah? A quarter?" A quarter would buy a brand new Spaldeen!

At the end of the hall they went into a large room with the words, "Bronx County Clerk's Office" on the door. Paul said hello to a woman whose gray hair was twisted into a bun and who was typing at a desk behind the counter. There were several offices, with men sitting at desks copying things from thick, black bound books. Against one wall were shelves filled with these books, which looked like you could copy stuff out of them for the rest of your life if you wanted to.

"What's in those books, Dad?"

"They give you information on the mortgages held against a particular property," Paul said. Freddy nodded, feeling a bit disappointed. It didn't sound too exciting.

Paul introduced Freddy to Si Berger, a curly-haired man with a quick smile, and Si said he might meet them later for lunch. As Paul was getting a chair for Freddy, a short, round man with glasses and a walrus moustache, who was sucking on a pipe, nodded and mumbled a greeting. Paul barely nodded in reply. He found a chair for Freddy in a quiet area. "Who was that guy with the moustache?" Freddy whispered.

"That's Joe Wolfe."

"Oh yeah? He's a friend of yours, isn't he?"

Paul's face tightened. "He used to be at one time."

"How come he isn't anymore?"

"I'll tell you later, Freddy. I have to get to work now."

"Is the boss watching you? Who is he?" Freddy persisted, hoping to keep Paul with him just a little longer in this cold, unfamiliar place.

Paul nodded toward a tall man with a red face and thin, sandy hair, who was talking to another man. "That's him over there, Larsen, the fellow in the blue suit." But the boss didn't look like anyone special at all.

"I'll see you later, Freddy. We'll be eating lunch at 11:30, but you should have enough to keep you busy until then. . . . The bathroom is at the end of the hall in case you need to use it." He tousled Freddy's hair, then strode briskly off. The big clock on the wall said five minutes after nine.

Freddy tried to read the sports page, but instead he kept thinking about Joe Wolfe with his big, fuzzy moustache. Freddy remembered Paul and Sarah once talking about Joe, saying something about his having 'turned sour.' So maybe Joe was on the side of the rich now. Even his name told you he was a bad guy. Freddy shuddered, hoping Joe wasn't going to do anything to Paul, maybe make him lose his job or go to jail.

Freddy turned to the *Times* crossword. He looked at it for a few moments, then sighed. It was a lot harder than those easy puzzles in his book; it wasn't fair, all those crazy words, stuff in foreign languages and Greek mythology. George would know all the mythology answers, of course. Oh well, Freddy would get the easy ones first, then the crazy ones later. But after over a half an hour's work, he'd gotten only a few words. Maybe Paul could help him out with a word or two; just a word or two wasn't really cheating. But Paul wasn't anywhere about. What had happened to him? Maybe Freddy wouldn't get to see the ballgame today. Finally he got up enough courage to ask about his father. The woman behind the counter said Paul was probably on the second floor copying things from the books up there. Freddy gave a sigh of relief. So there were even more of those darn books around!

It was five after eleven when Paul finally came by, carrying a bunch of papers. He helped Freddy with a few words, but by 11:30 Freddy hadn't gotten much further. He wondered how much of it George would have gotten. Paul held his manila folder, and his gray gabardine jacket was folded over the other arm. Freddy looked embarrassed.

"This was an especially tough one, even for the *Times*, I guess. I have trouble with some of them, too. . . . Come on, let's go to lunch," Paul beckoned.

It was sunny and hot outside. As they went down the steps, Freddy whispered, "How come you and Joe Wolfe aren't friends anymore?"

Paul mopped his face with a handkerchief. "Because he's a rat," he said in a low, hard voice. "At one time he used to be a halfway progressive guy, but now he's gotten cold feet. He wants to be on the boss' good side."

"How come?"

"Well, Larsen plays favorites. The guys who redbait get the easiest assignments, as well as the work when things are slow, while some of the rest of us might get laid off for awhile. That Larsen is just a lousy drunk. About all he does is sleep and read the paper and go home early."

"Can't they fire him for that?"

"He's palsy-walsy with all the cheap politicians. If it weren't for that, he'd get kicked out on his ass in no time."

Freddy sighed. When the smart people took over, then Paul would be put in charge; Larsen and Joe Wolfe would get fired, and maybe even thrown in jail for their crookedness. Freddy and Paul walked down to Jerome Avenue. The cafeteria was very crowded. Freddy eyed the food spread out on the counter. It never looked this good at home. Finally he settled on a meat loaf sandwich, a piece of apple pie, and a glass of lemonade. It was lucky Sarah wasn't here. She wouldn't have let him get the pie because of his broken-out face. A large-nosed, balding man in a white apron slapped Freddy's sandwich together. "Next!" the man boomed in a foghorn voice.

Paul ordered a chopped liver sandwich, and once again the man's thick, hairy hands did their magic. Paul paid the cashier, then carefully carried the tray toward a partially occupied table. Two older men wearing derby hats and sports clothes glanced up briefly from the horse racing section of the *Daily News*, then bent their heads back together again. Freddy and Paul exchanged knowing smiles as they sat down. Two morons betting money on a bunch of silly horses, Freddy thought, beginning to gobble his sandwich. If he was lucky, he'd see some of the batting practice before the game started.

"You don't have to eat so fast, Freddy. We have plenty of time," Paul advised, frowning at Freddy's rapidly disappearing sandwich.

"I'm hungry," Freddy mumbled, swallowing hard. He'd been too excited to eat much breakfast.

Si came over, removing a sandwich and cup of coffee from his tray, then sat down. He nodded toward the food line. "The three leading brains of the Bronx County Clerk's Office, Wolfe, Lazzeri, and Larsen, two fat *tucous* lickers and an alcoholic political hack."

Paul chuckled; Freddy glanced over and saw Joe Wolfe, Larsen, and another heavyset man standing and talking. "I was telling Freddy a little bit about Joe and Larsen, but I think Freddy's more interested in the ballgame today than in those characters. He hung around the whole morning just so we could go this afternoon," Paul said, smiling at Freddy.

"Who's going to win?" Si asked Freddy.

"The Yankees."

Si shook his head. "Y'know, if the Red Sox had Ted Williams now, they'd beat the Yanks. But Ted's off doing his patriotic duty, bombing the hell out of the Commies in Korea." Freddy glanced anxiously at the other two men, but they were still absorbed in their horse racing discussion.

"Yeah, Williams is a real bastard, all right," Paul agreed. "The Yankees and the Red Sox are probably the most reactionary outfits in the whole major leagues. They'll be the last ones, I bet, to have any Negroes on their teams. . . . The Yanks have so much damn money they've just about bought the pennant."

"Yeah, that's right," Si nodded, biting into his egg salad sandwich.

Freddy didn't say anything. He wondered whether being a Yankee fan made him just as bad as all the people who read the *Daily News* and those other crummy papers. If he'd lived in Brooklyn, though, he would have been a Dodger fan, so it wasn't altogether his fault. The Dodgers had a lot of good Negro players. Si and Paul began talking about property and mortgages, so Freddy didn't bother listening. He'd finished his food, and he shifted about in his chair, anxious to get going. Paul was slowly chewing his sandwich, like a cow. Freddy cursed his father's ulcers. If Paul didn't hurry up, maybe all the tickets would be sold out.

But finally Paul and Si finished eating, and Si went back to work while Freddy and Paul began walking to Yankee Stadium. The sun was bright and lazy; Freddy's blood raced. There were all those flags flying so it had to be real; it wasn't a dream. At the ticket window, Paul bought two bleacher tickets; he and Freddy made their way out to the seats in centerfield. Freddy felt a bit disappointed that the bleachers were just wooden benches and home plate looked so far off. But still, it was exciting feeling the stadium fill up in a vast, steady stream, even though it was just a weekday. The trim field, green, brown, and white, shone as if it were freshly painted. The Yankees were finishing up batting and fielding practice. It was better than television because you could watch everything going on all at once, even the players horsing around while they were practicing, though you couldn't hear what they were saying. A ripple of excitement went through Freddy each time he located one of his pinstriped heroes, Mickey Mantle, Yogi Berra, Phil Rizzuto, Billy Martin, Hank Bauer. So they were real, not just invented for television.

"When you were a kid, did you ever want to become a big league ballplayer?" Freddy asked.

"Sure, we all did. We used to play in Crotona Park, and there were a few guys who were pretty good and even played in the minors for awhile. . . . You know, Hank Greenberg used to come around sometimes, and he would pay me and some of the other guys to field and pitch batting practice to him. He was a big league prospect by then."

"Oh yeah?" Well, that was something, anyway, to have pitched batting practice to Hank Greenberg, since people in Freddy's family read books instead of becoming major league ballplayers.

Mickey Mantle, batting lefty, belted one into the right-field seats; the crowd buzzed. "Do you think Mantle's gonna be as good as Williams someday?" Freddy asked.

Paul's forehead creased in thought. "It's hard to say since it's only Mantle's second year. Right now he strikes out too much. He has to become much more consistent to reach Williams, who generally hits way over .300 every year." Freddy didn't say anything, though he was convinced in a few years Mantle would make people forget about Williams.

The starting pitchers were warming up near the dugouts now; Allie Reynolds, the burly Yankee righthander, was making the ball look like smoke. The rich aroma of mustard and hot dogs mingled with the smells of beer, peanuts, and sweat. Vendors, hopping about the seats like jack rabbits, called out their wares in voices that seemed to echo against the stadium walls. They were so mobbed with customers that Freddy felt a sense of accomplishment when he finally succeeded in exchanging his thirty cents for two ice cream pops.

Soon the warmups were over, and everyone stood for the National Anthem. A sudden hush fell over the stadium; the players stood lined up bareheaded alongside the dugouts, their caps placed over their hearts. It felt funny to see them without their caps, as if you were seeing now what they really looked like, Hank Bauer with his plastered down hair and tough face, or Mickey Mantle with his blonde crewcut over a round face and bull neck. Freddy smiled knowingly at his father. This was just as silly as pledging allegiance to the flag every morning at school. Everyone thought America was the greatest country in the whole world, but Paul and Freddy knew better, of course. The woman who sang the anthem had such a beautiful voice, though, that Freddy couldn't help his throat swelling up and his eyes moistening. Darn, the next thing you know he'd be reading the *Daily News*! He hoped Paul wouldn't notice anything. When the anthem was finished, there was a roar from the crowd, and Freddy shivered with excitement. The public address announcer read off the starting lineups, and Freddy marked his scorecard. Each of the Yankee players was cheered lustily, and the Red Sox ones booed by the crowd.

Allie Reynolds mowed the Sox down with his sliders and fastballs; lefty Mel Parnell baffled the Yanks with his big curve balls. Phil Rizzuto and Billy Martin came up with some snazzy fielding plays, but the Yanks weren't hitting. There was a muffled sigh of disappointment when Mantle went down swinging in the first inning. "You bum, Mickey!" someone called from several rows in back of Freddy. Mickey walked back to the dugout, his head sunk into his chest, as if he wanted to cry.

The Sox drew first blood in the fourth when Jimmy Piersall, the guy they said once used to be nuts, singled home Birdy Tebbetts. Freddy found himself wishing Piersall had stayed crazy. In the sixth Piersall was thrown out at the plate, and he threw his cap down and yelled at the umpire for awhile. Some of the other Red Sox joined in the argument, but the umpire wouldn't change his mind.

"He was out, wasn't he?" Freddy said.

Paul shrugged. "I don't know. It was very close. The umpires seem to be giving all the close ones to the Yankees, though." Freddy sighed, hoping Paul was wrong about the umps being on the Yanks' side.

In the bottom half of the sixth, Yogi Berra, who looked like a clown with his pancake ears and barrel body, lashed a single to right, tying the score. The fans clapped rhythmically as they stood for the seventh inning stretch, but Parnell set the Yanks down in order in the bottom half of the seventh. But in the eighth with two outs, Phil Rizzuto beat out an infield hit, and Billy Martin walked. Mickey stared at the ground as he advanced slowly toward the plate. He hadn't done much today, and there were more boos than cheers. The boos got even louder as he went down on one knee, missing the first pitch. The next one, though, he sent soaring toward left center. Freddy's heart beat wildly as the ball sailed over Piersall's outstretched glove. Mickey really made the dust fly around the basepaths. His powerful body churned into third standing up. There wasn't a boo in the whole stadium now. Tears came to Freddy's eyes, and he tried to blink them back so Paul wouldn't notice how silly he was. But even Paul seemed impressed. "Hmm, not bad," he nodded, smiling.

Protecting a 3-1 lead, Allie Reynolds got the first two batters in the top half of the ninth, but then Piersall walked, and Bobby Doerr sent him to second with a single to center. Vern Stephens was up, the Sox' big hitter now that Williams was away. Just one bad pitch, and the Sox would be leading. Casey Stengel, the Yanks' hunched old manager, shuffled out to the mound. "Leave him in, Case!" some of the fans shouted. Yogi, holding his catcher's mask, waddled out to the mound in his knee pads and chest protector. Case was moving his hands a lot as he talked, and Allie had his cap off and was mopping his forehead with his sleeve. Billy Martin and Phil Rizzuto came in from the infield to join the conference. When Case finally decided to leave Allie in the game, the fans cheered, and Freddy was glad, too, because Reynolds was the Yanks' best pitcher.

Stephens took his practice cuts, swinging hard. Allie was

careful with him, and the count got to three balls and one strike. Big Walt Dropo was up next. On the next pitch there was a loud crack; the ball sailed toward the wall in right center. Like everyone else, Freddy and Paul stood, craning their necks to see over the mass of other heads. They glimpsed Hank Bauer leaping against the wall, losing his cap as he speared the ball in the webbing of his glove just above his still perfect, pomaded hair. A roar filled the stadium; after a moment's hesitation, Freddy started clapping, too. He strained to see the broad grin on Bauer's cauliflower face that looked as if it had been chewed by a bear. Hank tossed the ball back toward the infield, jammed his cap back on, and began racing for the dugout to elude the fans already sprinkling out onto the field. Mantle shook hands with him, and they trotted side by side, Hank with arms and knees pumping in regular rhythm, Mickey with elbows swinging carelessly at his sides.

"That was quite a catch!"

Freddy nodded, a lump in his throat.

"We better get a move on," Paul urged. Freddy nodded again, straining to catch a last glimpse of Hank and Mickey disappearing into the dugout.

"Don't forget to take your jacket," Paul added.

Freddy put on his white cotton jacket. "That was a good game, wasn't it?" he finally said.

"It wasn't bad, but I think the Yankees were lucky to win. One or two calls the other way, and the Red Sox might have won."

Was Paul right? Maybe the rich Yankees had bought off all the umpires. Probably Joe Wolfe and Larsen liked the Yankees because they were crooked and reactionary. Freddy tried to tell Paul that maybe the Yankees weren't so hot, but the words refused to leave Freddy's throat. All right, he was a lousy reactionary. But then, maybe Paul was wrong about the Yankees and the umpires. That was possible, too.

Paul was looking at his watch. The crowd was moving toward the exits like a big, slow river. "It looks like we've gotten stuck this time. There's no telling when we'll get out of this place," Paul sighed. Freddy grinned. He didn't care if they got home after midnight.

Ralph Dranow was born in 1939 in the east Bronx, about a mile
from the Bronx Zoo, where he spent a good deal of his childhood
gaping at the animals. His other accomplishments include an illus-
trious career at Queens College, highlighted by membership on
the tennis team, which he represented ably, winning an occasional
match. In 1968 he decided to flee New York, following Horace
Greeley's adage: Go west, young man, go west. Ralph has lived
in the San Francisco Bay Area since 1970. He has held a wide
variety of jobs, such as Vista Volunteer in southeast Kentucky,
streetclub worker with gang members in NYC, stock clerk, and
temporary mailhandler at the Oakland Post Office. He is married
to Carla Kandinsky the poet and is the proud father of two
feisty felines, Schuss and Meatloaf.